TIPPLERS AND TEETOTALLERS

Or

What the Ancestors Drank

A social history of drinking from Mediaeval

times to the 21st century in Eastern Cornwall.

[Bodmin Moor to the Tamar]

Editor

Lynda Mudle-Small

© Callington Heritage Centre 2011

Callington Heritage Centre, Liskeard Road, Callington, PL17 7HA

E-mail enquiry@callingtonheritage.org.uk Web site www.callingtonheritage.org.uk

Contents

1. A Short History of Drinking in England   5
    By Miranda Lawrance Owen

2. A Quart of Beer and a Hogshead of Cider   15
    By Alastair Tinto and Nikki Chaplin

3. The Sober Alternative   21
    By Lynda Mudle-Small

4. Callington - The Town with Too Many Pubs   31
    By Lynda Mudle-Small

5. Parishes Without Pubs   45
    By Miranda Lawrance-Owen

6. A Taste for the Low and Vulgar   51
    By Nikki Chaplin

7. Drinking in St. Dominick   65
    by Alastair Tinto

8. The Village Inn   73
    By Miranda Lawrance-Owen and Lynda Mudle-Small

    Index   81

Acknowledgements

First I must thank my co-authors for their valuable contributions to this book. Nikki Chaplin, Miranda Lawrance-Owen and Alastair Tinto have all proven that there is nothing like local knowledge when it comes to local history. It has been a pleasure to work with them and the opportunity to bounce ideas back and forth as well as information and data sources has been mutually beneficial. We have all made use of local archives, such as the Callington Heritage Centre, Calstock Archive Trust and the Stoke Climsland Archive and this emphasises the need for such depositories of local information and the importance of the work that many volunteers do in keeping these centres functioning. Various items from these archives have been acknowledged throughout the book and in the endnotes.

Local archives and local people are also a valuable source of photographs. With historic photographs it is always difficult to identify the holder of the copyright as the donor of the photograph may not necessarily hold the copyright. All reasonable efforts have been made to trace the copyright holder of material and photographs in this book. Any untraced claimant of copyright should contact myself so that amendments can be made in the next edition. As with many older photographs, I regret that the quality is not what I could wish for and I apologise for this, however I have made the decision to include them in the belief that the information they contain should be perpetuated even if the quality is poor.

I personally must thank the Callington U3A history group for compiling some of the initial information on Callington inns. From their information numerous visits have been made to the Cornish Studies Library, the Cornwall Record Office, the Courtney Library [Royal Cornwall Museum] and Liskeard Library. I and my co-authors have always found the staff at these centres to be courteous and helpful.

Lynda Mudle-Small
June 2011

Notes:
There are numerous references to newspaper articles which are indicated by superscript:

CT	Cornish Times
SM	Sherborne and Yeovil Mercury
GAZ	Royal Cornwall Gazette
WB	West Briton

These newspapers can all be accessed at the Cornish Studies Library in Redruth.
Superscript is also used for some common sources:

PR	Parish Registers
CS	Census returns
DY	Street or Postal Directory

Published by Callington Heritage Centre ISBN 978-0-9561819-1-6
Callington Heritage Centre, Liskeard Road, Callington, Cornwall, PL17 7HA.
Tel: www.callingtonheritage.org.uk E-mail enquiry@callingtonheritage.org.uk
Cover painting donated by Anthea Lay, who can be contacted via the Heritage Centre.

CHAPTER 1

A Short History of Drinking in England

By Miranda Lawrance-Owen

The history of public drinking and drinking places in England is a long one stretching from the roadside 'mansiones' and 'tabernae' of the Romans, via mediaeval inns, alehouses and taverns and the great coaching inns of the eighteenth and nineteenth centuries to the enormous variety of cafes, coffee shops, pubs, hotels, bars and other licensed premises which we have today.

The overall picture is one of a struggle between the ruling elites, attempting to impose their notions of order and morality, and the poorer and less powerful members of society, attempting to continue with ways of life which they never regarded as a problem.

Traditionally, the three types of public drinking places were the inn, the alehouse and the tavern, all of which date back to the mediaeval period. The primary purpose of inns was the provision of hospitality for travellers and the law placed obligations on innkeepers to look after travellers and their goods.[1] Alehouses were primarily drinking places, although many also supplied food and sometimes lodgings and there was considerable overlap between alehouses and inns. Taverns also provided accommodation. Their distinguishing feature was that technically they sold only wine, not ale.

The term 'pub' seems to have become common from around the mid Victorian era.

The Early History of Drinking: 700 - 1485

It is difficult to discover much detail about English drinking habits and attitudes before the fifteenth century but we have a few tantalising glimpses of that vanished world, mainly through the laments of the church authorities about excessive drinking. When Christianity came to Britain in the sixth century it succeeded largely by absorbing and reshaping old pagan traditions. Many of these centred on drinking, therefore drinking became a central part of English Christianity and of English community life. Reading between the lines of the complaints by the early authorities we get an idea of what was happening in towns and villages across England. As early as 616 Ethelbert, King of Kent, attempted to regulate the number of alehouses and In 745 Ecbright, Archbishop of York gave orders that no drinking should be done in church and tried to stop priests from entering taverns for food or drink, declaring that "no priest should be an ale sop". He also urged people to be "very temperate at Church wakes and pray earnestly [that] there be no drinking

or unseemliness".[2] A great deal of drinking clearly went on amongst priests and by all sorts of people in and around churches.

Despite Ethelbert's attempts to control the number of alehouses they appear to have multiplied and three hundred years later excessive drinking was still perceived to be a problem. In 975, King Edgar attempted to restrict the number of alehouses per village to one and tried to standardise alehouse drinking vessels to four pints, known as a 'pottle'. Each pottle had to be subdivided into eight parts by pegs fixed inside the tankard and no one was to drink down further than one peg at a sitting. It seems that this backfired completely as mediaeval English alehouse customers invented a new drinking game of 'taking each other down a peg or two'. [Manners required not drinking more than your allotted peg because if you took more this short changed the next drinker. If you did so you therefore had to finish the next peg as well to leave him a clear peg worth of ale.] Ancient Welsh chronicles record that British chieftains always went into battle drunk. Amongst other things they tell us that before the Battle of Hastings in 1066 the Normans spent the night in prayer and contemplation but the Saxons had been drinking hard to celebrate their victory at Stamford Bridge and "were no better than drunk when they came to fight".[3]

In the mediaeval period the church was usually the only large building in the community and the nave of the Church was the people's communal meeting place and place of celebration as well as the place for their Sunday worship. Despite Ecbright's demands in 745, drinking in churches continued:

An illustration from the 14th century Luttrell Psalter [an illuminated manuscript]. The exact meaning of the figures is obscure but this seems to illustrate some drunken revellery

the tenth century Archbishop, Aelfric, complained that "men often act so absurdly as to sit up all night and drink to madness within God's house and defile it with scandalous and lewd discourse".[4] Historians seem to agree that the mediaeval church was heavily involved in communal feasting and celebration. Churches were also major contributors to the production of ale through 'Church Ales' which were a regular feature of life.

All this would no doubt have been going on in Cornwall during the middle ages in the same way as in other parts of the country. We get a picture of Cornish church ales from various sources. Churchwardens' accounts from Launceston, Bodmin, and eight other Cornish churches in the period 1461 – 1559 reveal that income for the maintenance of churches came mostly from voluntary contributions by parishioners including money raised at "convivial feasts known as church ales". Originally these took place in the church but by the late Middle Ages such events had became so important that some parishes erected a special building known as a "Church House" where church ales and other functions could take place.[5] One of the best surviving examples is at Poundstock.

The church hierarchy regularly attempted to prohibit such events, particularly when they were held in the church. For example, the perhaps unfortunately named Bishop Brewer of Exeter [Exeter Diocese included Cornwall until the nineteenth century] forbade the holding of "scotales", or church ales, in churches in his diocese in the early thirteenth century.[6]

Despite this, church ales were still being held in Cornwall as late as 1602 Carew gives a detailed description of the process whereby two young men of the parish were chosen each year to collect money from parishioners to be used for "brewing baking and other provisions" and then at Whitsuntide and other holidays parishioners and people from neighbouring parishes would meet at the Church House for the celebration. Money raised at the church ale was then presented by the young men for the upkeep of the church.[7] Carew also reports, however, that many clergy had begun to suppress church ales as being "licentious". Carew himself clearly thought the practice should be ended: "the very title of ale was somewhat nasty, and the thing itself had been corrupted with such a multitude of abuses, to wit, idleness, drunkenness, lasciviciousness, vain disports of minstrelsy, dancing, and disorderly night watchings"![8]

Despite, or perhaps because of, the involvement of the church, attempts at regulation of drinking continued. However, there was an increasing conflict for the authorities between their desire to control drunkenness and considerations such as the need to ensure essential supply and as time went on, a desire to maintain income through fines and taxation. Ale had become a necessity by the late Middle Ages because pollution from trades such as butchers and tanners meant that water was not safe to drink and everyone therefore drank ale instead. There was no real alternative, even for women and children, until the end of the eighteenth century.

Cornish ale apparently had a bad name and one contemporary described it as looking "as if pygges had wrastteled in it".[9]

Alehouses had become common throughout the country by the beginning of the fourteenth century and most brewed their own ale for sale on the premises. Ale could be bought in quantity from 'common brewers' to be sold in inns or 'tipling houses'. [In general, tipling houses merely sold drink whereas alehouse keepers brewed their own on the premises. In practice the two terms seem to have been used interchangeably.] Brewing or selling to supplement the income of a poor family may also have been common.[10] Many ale houses would have been ordinary domestic dwellings and although some of the more permanent ones may have provided food or even lodgings,

The church house at Poundstock

they usually just provided drink. Early alehouses were often very transient places and hard to identify in the historical record.

Intolerable Hurts and Troubles:
the struggle for 'Order' and 'Godliness' 1485-1660

In an echo of the concerns of the church hierarchy in the years before the Norman Conquest, alehouses and the drunkenness of the lower orders were becoming more and more of a concern to the elite by the time the Tudor monarchs came to the throne. As early as 1495 Henry VII, in an act concerned with vagabonds and beggars, gave justices of the peace power to suppress alehouses, and in 1552, during the reign of Edward VI, the first licensing act in the modern sense was passed. The preamble to this act referred to the "intolerable Hurts and Troubles to the Commonwealth of this realm caused by common Alehouses and other Houses called Tipling Houses".[11] The act introduced the requirement for alehouses to be licensed and gave power to two justices of the peace to issue and renew licences and to withdraw licences from any alehouse or tipling house, which in the opinion of the justices was not well kept. The requirement to obtain a justices licence was soon extended to inns, leaving only the taverns, which traded under crown licence until 1792, outside local jurisdiction. The long involvement of local justices of the peace with regulating public drinking had begun.

The attempts of the Reformation monarchs to control drinking were fuelled both by concern about the perceived threat of unrest by the 'lower orders' and by the desire to curb the 'ungodly activities' of the church and some of its practices. This led, amongst other things, to the suppression of church ales and the final severing of the link between the church and drunken feasting. An unintended consequences of this was the lessening of the part played by the Church in community life. Once churches were no longer the centre of communal celebrations, this made room for alehouses and inns to assume a wider role than that of mere drinking houses or hospitality for travellers. They became the common gathering place, the focus for news and gossip and the new place for communal celebration of events such as weddings. As time went on they became centres of "local administration in politics, the places where feasts and banquets were held and where the county and urban gentry met for social and intellectual activities ranging from cockfighting to lectures and debates".[12]

The first reasonably reliable indication of the numbers of inns and alehouses in England comes from a government survey of 1577, carried out in an attempt to discover the numbers of places available for billeting soldiers. Based on that survey, it has been estimated that across England and Wales there were approximately 3,600 inns, about 24,000 alehouses and a much smaller number of taverns. Certificates have survived for four out of the nine Cornish administrative divisions known as hundreds.[13] They reveal a total of 132 alehouses and 30 taverns, but interestingly no inns are recorded. This may be because the terms were used fairly loosely and inns may have been included in the totals of both alehouses and taverns. Alternatively inns, in the sense of establishments superior to alehouses, may indeed have been few in number at that time. Carew says that "strangers travelling through the Shire were wont to inveigh against the bad drink, coarse lodging and slack attendance they found in those houses that went for inns" and suggests that this was mainly because 'wayfarers' at that time were few and people thought there was little point spending good money in a vain attempt to attract them.[14] John Norden, the mapmaker, who travelled through Cornwall in about 1584 supported this view saying that "the ordinarie provisions in these places are very meane".[15] Both suggest that anyone who was anyone would lodge with gentry friends and relations instead.

If the total alehouses in the four western hundreds are averaged and applied to the remaining five eastern hundreds, we can estimate that there would have been a total of about three hundred alehouses across Cornwall and about thirty three in the Hundred of East which includes Callington and surrounding parishes. The population of Cornwall at that time has been estimated to be a little under 100,000 and the population of Callington about 250 to 300.[16]

Despite continuing attempts to control drinking, alcohol consumption apparently increased and some commentators suggest that by the reign of James 1, from 1603, drunkenness was rife among all classes and that "there was no social stigma attached to getting drunk".[17] No less than five acts of parliament attempted to control drunkenness between 1604 and 1627. The mediaeval principle that the innkeeper was responsible for the behaviour of his guests came to an end in 1606 when, for the first time, the individual drunkard could be fined or put in the stocks. Licences could be revoked for the offence of keeping a drunken house and local officials were required to act as informers. In 1627 parish authorities were permitted to administer public flogging to those who did not pay their fines and, as an incentive for a parish to enforce the law, the fines could be used to supplement the parish poor rate.

During the civil war and the Commonwealth many alehouses were closed and almost all the traditional leisure pastimes of the people were outlawed most of which, of course, would have revolved around drinking. However, in the backlash which followed the Restoration of the monarchy in 1660, drunkenness was unsurprisingly perceived to be on the increase again, and in 1660 Charles II felt obliged to publish a 'Proclamation Against Drunkenness'.

The eighteenth century: conflicting attitudes and continuing concern

Increasing control by justices of the peace, combined with aspirations to greater respectability on the part of alehouse keepers, gradually led to alehouses providing better facilities and during the eighteenth century the description 'alehouse' slowly began to be superseded by the description 'public house'. There remained a distinct hierarchy of drinking places although there was still an overlap between different types and in different areas of the country. At the top were the large inns of major towns, sometimes called 'hotel' by the middle of the eighteenth century. Next came the humbler inns of towns such as Callington. These would have had a 'tap' room, at least one parlour and some accommodation for travellers. At the bottom of the hierarchy were the alehouses, the drinking places of the 'lower orders'. These mostly had just the 'tap' room and sometimes an additional parlour or private room. The modern bar did not develop until the end of the eighteenth century. At that time the bar was a room used as an office and valuables store.

The biggest change on the English drinking scene occurred in the mid eighteenth century when gin became widely available. Its sale went up from about half a million gallons in 1689 to over seven million gallons by the 1750s.[18] The main reason for this was that the selling of gin was not restricted by the requirement to obtain a Justices licence and could be sold by anyone from individual streetwalkers or small one-room spirit shops to coffee houses and existing licensed premises. It was even sold in prisons and workhouses. By the 1750s, about half of all alehouses, inns and taverns also sold spirits. The Plymouth Gin Company was founded in 1793 and Plymouth apparently had so many gin shops by 1802 that a naval surgeon by the name of Thomas Trotter claimed to have been instrumental in the closure of as many as two hundred of them. [Thomas Trotter later became the first person to develop the idea of heavy drinking as a disease].[19]

Even in Cornwall, where smuggled brandy might have been expected to be more common than gin, Peter Bray of Liskeard was accused in 1749 of "frequenting gin shops on Sundays during Divine service".[20] The 'gin craze' had clearly penetrated South East Cornwall too. Eventually, in 1792, both gin shops and taverns were brought under the jurisdiction of local justices of the peace.

In contrast to the continuing concerns of the establishment about the drinking habits of the lower orders, it was during the eighteenth and early nineteenth centuries that inns and public houses became central to the administrative, economic and social life of the country. There were almost no public buildings at that time, so Justices' licensing sessions were themselves frequently held at inns, as were public meetings, coroners courts and of course public and private celebrations of all sorts. Inns were also vital to the growing transport network, as a result of which the number of inns had gone up to about twenty thousand by 1750, roughly three times the number which existed fifty years earlier.[21]

The earlier figures for numbers of inns and alehouses are estimates. However, after 1808 licensed publicans also had to obtain an excise licence to sell beer and the centrally maintained excise records are fairly complete. By 1829 there was a total of 50,442 licensed premises, about one to every 276 inhabitants in the country.[22]

The Victorian Era: more of the same?

Anxiety about the drinking habits of the lower classes continued unabated into the Victorian era. There were many strands to this by the nineteenth century, including the threat to the health and therefore usefulness of the poor as workers, soldiers or mothers;[23] the perceived link between drunkenness and crime; fear of increasing general disrespect for authority and perceptions of the breakdown of home and family life. Throughout the nineteenth century the authorities continued to attempt to reduce the number of alehouses and in some cases this merged with attempts to reform the behaviour of the lower classes.

Running counter to this was a growing movement to free the licensing system. There was widespread complaint by publicans about abuse of magisterial discretion and about increasing control of public houses by breweries. The publicans' complaints became linked with the wider free trade movement and in 1830, an 'Act To Permit the General Sale of Beer and Cyder by Retail' ['the Beer Act'] introduced a new type of drinking establishment, that of the beer shop. Beer shop proprietors obtained their licence direct from the excise and were thus separate from the control of local magistrates. Such a development appeared to run completely contrary to the establishment disapproval of working-class behaviour and the anti-drink approach which had gone before and there was, as might have been expected, considerable opposition. That the act was passed seems to have had more to do with the particular situation of the Duke of Wellington's administration than the strength of the publicans' case, even when this was allied to the free trade movement, but for the next forty years beer houses, beer shops [or 'kidleywinks' as they were known in Cornwall and the Midlands] operated alongside alehouses, pubs and inns. The proprietors of these new establishments variously appear in the censuses and other historical records as 'beer house [or beer shop] keeper', 'beerseller' or 'retailer of beer'. Often, however, they do not appear at all in the records. Beer shops were commonly carried on alongside other occupations or were run by the proprietors' wives and only the main, or perhaps more 'respectable', occupation would be given. The growth of beer shops was rapid – in the first year 31,937 excise licences were issued, 26,291 of them in the first three months. At the same time the excise records show that the total number of ordinary licensed publicans, [innkeepers and alehouse keepers] was 50,547. More than one in three drink retailers were now beer shops and instead of there being one drink retailer for every two hundred and seventy six inhabitants of the country there was now one for every one hundred and sixty eight people.[24]

Contemporary commentators began complaining almost immediately about the increased drunkenness created by beer shops. Within four months of the passing of the act the Royal Cornwall Gazette was reporting that "a great deal of mischief has lately been done ... by the drunken frequenters of cheap beer shops".[25] In the years that followed, the papers are full of similar reports and complaints. The backlash was rapid and in Truro, for example, a Temperance Society was formed as early as April 1832. Callington's Temperance Society was formed in 1839. Concerns centred once again on the class origins of beer shop proprietors and their customers, together with the perceived connection with drunkenness, immorality and crime.

The Plymouth Gin distillery, founded in 1793, is in the Barbican, one of the oldest parts of the city.

There is no doubt that the Beer Act was responsible for an enormous increase in numbers of licensed premises, but not as many as contemporary commentators made out. After 1837 the numbers of beer shops fell close to the first year's figure and thereafter only rose slowly until a surge in the mid 1860s.[26] A few changes were made during that time: beer shop keepers were required to obtain a certificate of good character, signed by six rated [and therefore not the poorest] residents of the parish and certified by one of the parish overseers before the excise would grant a licence. In addition, a qualifying rateable value was introduced for all beer shops. The legislation was confusing and allegations of evasion were rife. In Callington for example, at the Petty Sessions of July 1859 a case against one Henry Bullen, a beer shop keeper accused of keeping late hours, was dismissed, "it appearing that he did it ignorantly, believing from the regulations laid down by the Board of Excise in cases of rating and population, that he was authorised in keeping his house open to 11 o'clock".[CT]

Many beer shop proprietors had aspirations to greater respectability and subsequently applied for full justices licences for their beer shops or moved to become licensees of existing pubs. The census records reveal the same attitudes and aspirations, many beer shop proprietors listing themselves as 'publican' or 'innkeeper' instead.

Eventually, in 1869, the free trade experiment came to an end and the Wine and Beerhouse Act brought beerhouses under the control of local magistrates. The "little clumps of squires and parsons",[27] were in full charge once again and the results were almost immediate. Many beer shops were refused licences at the next licensing sessions and by 1871 the number of beer houses had fallen back by almost fifteen percent to 42,950.[28]

One major change which seems to have been stimulated by the desire of the 'better sort' of establishments to distance themselves from the lowly beer shop was the change in pub architecture introduced first in the great 'gin palaces' of London and other large cities. Although the 'gin palace' was mainly an urban phenomenon, architectural changes took place all over the country, the most notable of which was probably the introduction into pubs of the over counter service which we think of as the 'traditional' pub bar.

Another driver of change was the "improved public house movement".[29] of the late nineteenth century which arose out of the temperance movement. The idea was that improvements to public houses and provision of non alcoholic beverages as well as alcohol, would improve drinking habits, particularly those of the lower classes. In general, justices of the peace seem to have gone along with this strategy, requiring improvements to be made as a condition of licence renewal. Local examples appear in newspaper reports of the Callington Licensing Sessions, objectors wanted Sarah Hicks' beer house in Henwood closed in September 1874[CT], for example, because the house was of low rateable value and not up to standard. The renewal was granted only after she accepted the improvement conditions imposed on her licence.

Despite all the changes, drinking patterns in the mid Victorian era seem in many ways to mirror those of the preceding three centuries. There was still a hierarchy of different establishments, frequented in varying numbers by all classes of society, within a context of continued concern by the middle and upper classes about drunkenness, immorality and potential unrest among the lower classes. The respectable classes, particularly women, were perhaps beginning to frequent drinking establishments less, but overall, opportunities for drinking and attitudes towards drink remained much as they had always been.

Brewery control and declining fortunes

The rise of brewery companies changed the position considerably for many publicans. In the early 1700s almost seventy percent of publicans brewed their own beer, but by 1900 the number had fallen to less than four percent.

During the eighteenth and early nineteenth centuries many innkeepers had become men of substance and alehouse keepers of the 'better sort' were also becoming wealthier and more respectable. A public house in a good position became an attractive business proposition not only for individuals but also for brewery companies. On the other hand, for the smaller establishments or those not in a very good position, particularly small alehouses or beer shops, the situation was not as rosy. The census and licensing records show that many proprietors moved out of the business altogether thus creating opportunities for the breweries to buy up their pubs.

These opportunities increased as the century progressed. By the late nineteenth century, contrary to the perceptions of many, alcohol consumption was declining and the public house no longer occupied the central role in society it had previously held. Increased disposable income, improved housing conditions and the growing amount of alternative leisure opportunities such as the music hall, and mass spectator sports all detracted from the popularity of the pub as the hub of social life. As the profits to be gained from pubs decreased, bankruptcies became common and pubs were frequently bought up by the brewing companies. By the turn of the century more and more pubs across the country were owned or leased by a brewery

company and the publican was a tenant. The Licensing Act of 1904 introduced a mechanism for removing pubs considered by the magistrates to be redundant and records of licensing proceedings at that time confirm that many publicans were struggling to convince local magistrates that they were viable.

Ownership of pubs by family owned breweries gradually gave way to larger concerns. Tamar Breweries and Plymouth Breweries bought up pubs in the Callington area towards the end of the nineteenth century. These breweries, in turn were swallowed up by larger concerns such as Courage Breweries.

On the other hand, it was not all bad news for pubs. They remained a central institution in the lives of working-class men well into the twentieth century. They also continued to function as meeting places for all sorts of events from local auctions to friendly society meetings and in this capacity attracted all classes of person. They remained important for trade and communications too and carrier services continued to be based at pubs until well into the twentieth century. General hospitality functions also continued to bring in custom. Many pubs in the late nineteenth and early twentieth centuries still offered coffee and hot meals. For many workmen the pub was the equivalent of the works canteen and pubs often allowed customers to eat their own food on the premises or would even cook it for them.

The late nineteenth and early twentieth-centuries: JPs, policing and political control

Not only did local magistrates regulate public drinking through their control of the licensing system but they also dealt with the full range of drink and licence related offences including individual drunkenness, disorderly alehouses, selling without a licence and opening outside permitted hours, etc. However, the records suggest that until the mid nineteenth century there was very little overall increase in court cases, despite the increasingly vociferous concern of the establishment about drunkenness and the behaviour of the lower orders. The reason for this is not hard to find when one considers that until the middle of the nineteenth century law enforcement depended on local parish constables. These were unpaid ordinary members of the community, usually from the artisan, trade or farming classes, who would have been subject not only to pressure from the communities in which they lived but also to their own personal opinions which might not have been antagonistic towards alehouses and inns. Even if the constables were assiduous in carrying out their duties, it was very difficult to find any witnesses willing to come forward to testify against their local alehouse innkeeper. This would have been particularly the case in rural areas such as Callington and the surrounding districts. One witness to a Parliamentary commission commented that "there are not many people who like to turn informers in country places".[30]

In 1856 professional policing was introduced for the whole country[31] and this immediately led to more efficient supervision of drinking establishments. Successful prosecutions were still difficult - publicans and their customers frequently placed lookouts to watch for the approach of the police, and there remained the old problem of persuading customers to give evidence against their local publican. From the evidence which does survive, it appears that opening in prohibited hours was probably the most common offence.

The 1872 Licensing Act eventually codified the numerous offences which might be committed by a licence holder and increased the various penalties. From then on offences were recorded on the licence and repeated conviction was one of the grounds for forfeiture. Opening outside permitted hours continued to be the commonest offence, but although policing became more efficient, the number of cases brought before the justices throughout the country continued to fall. This has led many commentators to conclude that the running of pubs and the behaviour of their

customers was improving.[32] The danger of losing a licence as a result of convictions, combined with the considerable profits being made by some publicans, meant that for the first time there was real incentive for publicans to remain within the law. Furthermore, many pubs were now owned by large brewery businesses which did not look favourably on tenants who risked convictions. In Callington the magistrates must have been very pleased with developments – at the Sessions in September 1880 it was reported that Superintendent Barnes had "brought before them during the year about 26 cases of drunkenness, about the same as the previous year. He had no objection to a single house".[CT] All the licences were renewed and there were no new applications.

By contrast, the statistics show that proceedings against individuals for drunkenness began to increase during the final years of the nineteenth century.[33] However, as there was no legal definition of drunkenness at that time the decision to prosecute must have been somewhat arbitrary and very much subject to the individual views of the local police and magistrates. Increasing numbers of proceedings for drunkenness do not therefore necessarily mean that drunkenness was on the increase in any given area.

Successive governments throughout the nineteenth and early twentieth centuries were certainly concerned to limit excessive drinking, but this was always in conflict with their interest in the revenue brought in through taxation of the drink trade. Overall however, establishment opinion combined with pressure from the temperance movement does seem to have been successful in gradually reducing excessive drinking. The licensing act of 1872 not only increased the likelihood of licences not being renewed as a result of previous breaches of the law but also made it more difficult to obtain a new licence and overall the number of licensed premises was falling. There is no doubt that magistrates were actively pursuing a policy of suppression. Magistrates at Farnham in Surrey refused to renew all forty-five licences in Farnham and eventually succeeded in permanently depriving six pubs of their licences.[34] Other areas followed their example and as a result of this case more licences were denied renewal in 1903 than in the previous six years combined. At the Callington sessions in March 1903 objections were made to the renewal of licences of nine pubs in the area. There were no real objections on the grounds of the conduct of the landlords, all were put forward for closure solely in an attempt to reduce the number of licensed premises. In the end only one was closed, but most of the others had conditions imposed on their licences. [CT]

Unsurprisingly, publicans and the brewery companies were furious about this and in 1904 the

A Plymouth Breweries advertisement from a trade directory of 1895

new Conservative administration under Balfour introduced a scheme of compensation [funded by the brewing trade] where licences were refused on grounds other than misconduct.

The First World War and beyond: into the twenty-first century

The First World War marked a turning point in the nation's alcohol consumption. One obvious reason was tax increases and the generalised price rises of the war, both of which caused the price of beer and spirits to soar. However, other factors also played a part. Concern about the effects of drink on servicemen and war work led to the creation in May 1915 of the Central Control Board [of Liquor Traffic] which was given powers to 'increase the efficiency of labour and prevent drunkenness alcoholism or excess'. The nation as a whole was also exhorted to consume less in order to help the war effort. Lloyd George declared that "drink is doing us more damage in the war than all the German submarines put together".[35] and George V set an example by declaring that he would abstain from alcohol for the whole of the war.

However, the government also accepted that moderate social drinking could be a good support for morale. The provision of food in pubs and the sale of lower alcohol beers was encouraged [English beer never regained its pre-war strength]. The overall effect of the activities of the Board, combined with the fact that women workers with more money to spend were increasingly frequenting pubs, seems to have been that pubs became more respectable places where responsible drinking was the norm.

The downward trend in alcohol consumption brought about during the First World War continued throughout the twentieth century, apart from a brief increase during the Second World War. By 1955, per capita consumption of beer was down to twelve gallons per year[36] and consumption did not rise again until the very end of the twentieth and beginning of the twenty-first century.[37]

There were also major changes to the appearance of pubs during the course of the twentieth century both internally and externally. Such changes had been encouraged originally by the temperance and 'improved public house' movement and were continued during the First World War by the Central Control Board, keen to push the idea that improvements to public houses and the encouragement of women and families by the provision of brighter premises would lead to improved drinking habits. From the point of view of the survival of the pub as an institution, the movement for improvement appears to have succeeded. Although the number of on-licences in England and Wales fell by fifteen percent between

1951 and 1971, by the end of the century pubs had once again become central to the social activities of the nation and the turnover of pubs as a whole rose in real terms.[38]

By the beginning of the twenty-first century even the decline in the numbers of drinking establishments seems to have been reversed. This appears to be largely due to the Licensing Act of 2003 which brought to an end almost half a century of control of pubs by local justices of the peace. Under the 2003 act, all responsibility for licensing was transferred to local authorities and in a major shift of policy they were required to grant all applications unless objections were received. The effects appear to have been immediate. By 2004 the number of on-licences had risen by twenty percent to 81,455.[39]

However, this numerical increase conceals some rapid and dramatic changes. Pubs may once again be a major part of the social life of all classes of society but the number of 'traditional' pubs is declining. New pubs are rare and today's new licensed premises are unlikely to be aimed at a cross section of the community but are more likely to be modern bars or clubs aimed particularly at younger people.

Who ran pubs?

The proprietors of early drinking establishments were men and women from all walks of life below the gentry. In the larger inns, innkeepers such as the Golding family of Callington often became men of wealth and substance whereas alehouse keeping and beer shop keeping were generally the preserve of the lower classes, from farmers and craftsmen downwards. It was common for another occupation to be carried on alongside that of drink retailing. Between 1650 and 1777 thirty one different 'by-employments' out of one hundred and thirty nine alehouse keepers have been identified. A third of these were farmers and farming was still a very important by-employment at the time of the 1851 Census. After farmers, the next largest by-trades were those of craftsmen, retailers and dealers. Dual occupations remained common in rural areas late into the nineteenth century, as can be seen from later chapters of this book.[40]

If the licensee pursued another occupation, it was usually his wife who ran the pub and even where innkeeping was the sole occupation wives were regarded as essential business partners. There were also significant numbers of women running pubs on their own, usually widows of a deceased publican. It was not unusual for male publicans to 'die on the job'. Innkeeping was frequently a family affair - in addition to the wife, census records often reveal the involvement of children or other relatives. Larger establishments might also employ a number of servants. Census descriptions of barmaid or barman are uncommon until the later census reports from about 1901. Until then many pub employees were simply recorded as 'servant'. The origin of the description barmaid or barman is not known but in view of the fact that the bar was originally the private office of the publican and the place where valuables were kept and accounts were done it may once have been a higher status post than it subsequently became.[41]

Although routes into the trade for new licence holders were varied, experience seems to have been important from the earliest years, particularly in the 'better sort' of establishment. Many moved from another inn or had been in service at an inn. Others moved from household service – in Callington, for example, William Porter of the *Bull's Head* 1771 was "late servant of Sir John St. Aubyn" and William Golding 1816 was "late servant to the Rev. Ed. Clarke of St. Dominic".[42]

After the introduction of beer shops in 1830 beer shop keeping became a popular route into fully licensed premises and many men became beer shop keepers in the hope of moving up the hierarchy. A final common route into the trade was from occupations from which men retired early such as sport, the military or, in later years, the police.[43] For example Richard Pethick of the *Farmers Arms* Golberdon was a naval pensioner and George Solomon of the *Sun Inn* [*Coryton Arms*] St. Mellion was a former policeman,

Who were the customers?

Overall, the majority of pub customers have always been men and predominantly men from the working classes. However, within this generalisation there have been many variations over the years. During the seventeenth century, following the establishment of inns as vital for travellers and as important centres of local economic and social activity, there was considerable patronage by the upper and middle classes and this only began to decline after the mid-nineteenth century with the demise of the coaching trade and increasing concern about the 'evils of drink' within 'respectable' society. Numerically, however, the middle and upper classes were always outnumbered as customers by skilled workers, small craftsmen and petty traders.

Not only was there a hierarchy between establishments, there was also a hierarchy within establishments: the gentry and other 'respectable classes' would always have remained apart from the 'lower orders' and the craftsmen, farmers and tradesmen who patronised inns at which their social inferiors also drank would congregate in the private room or parlour leaving the tack room for the semi or unskilled 'lower orders'.

Perhaps surprisingly, women were also to be found in pubs from the earliest times although in far smaller numbers than men and rarely unaccompanied by men until the early eighteenth century and the arrival of the 'gin craze'. 'Respectable society' seems always to have viewed the issue of women drinking as a cause for concern on the basis that they were the mothers of the nation's future workers and soldiers. By the Victorian era this had become both a moral and a nationalistic issue with the growing ideal that a woman's place was in the home and the view that mothers were responsible for the 'the future of the Empire'.[44]

As far as children were concerned, it was not until 1908 that children under fourteen were banned from the bars of licensed premises. The first act which made any reference at all to children and alcohol came in 1839 when it became illegal to sell spirits for consumption by children under sixteen. This only applied in London and did not become law across the rest of the country until 1872. The ban was not extended to other drinks until 1886 when it became illegal to sell any form of alcoholic drink to children under thirteen. It was after the First World War, in 1923, that legislation was eventually passed prohibiting the sale of alcohol to anybody under the age of eighteen.

Opening hours

Historically, alehouses and inns could open at any time except during the hours of church services. This was only formalised in 1828 at which time opening on Good Friday and Christmas Day were also prohibited. The Beer Act of 1830 made it illegal for beer shops to remain open after one o'clock in the morning and this principle was eventually extended to all types of licensed premises throughout the country in 1848. The 1848 Act also limited opening times on Sundays: there was to be no opening before 12.30 and pubs had to be closed between 3 p.m. and 5 p.m.

Probably the most dramatic changes to pub opening hours came about as a result of the First World War and were continued under the Licensing Act of 1921 which established the twentieth century pattern: pubs could no longer open in the early morning or during mid-afternoon and they had to be closed by 11 o'clock at night. This remained the case until 2003 when the same act which removed control of licensing from local magistrates[45] allowed applications for consent to extend opening hours beyond 11pm. However, despite considerable opposition to the idea and lamentations about the onset of 'twenty four hour drinking' few establishments apart from clubs and larger new establishments have applied for extended hours, and pubs in general still close at 11pm.

How much did people really drink?

Levels of alcohol consumption remained high long after the seventeenth century. It has been estimated that in the early 1700s weekly consumption per head was about twelve to sixteen pints. Some of this was the 'small beer' drunk by women, children and servants and men's consumption could have been much higher. By the 1750s labourers were apparently drinking about four pints of strong beer per day and large quantities of gin and other spirits were being consumed by many people.

By the early 1800s consumption in public drinking establishments, excluding drinking in the home, is still believed to have been over five pints of beer a week per head of population and, with a few fluctuations, this went up in the second half of the nineteenth century to over six pints per head. After making allowances for children, abstainers and lower female consumption of beer, male consumption in the late nineteenth century has been estimated at between eleven and twelve pints per week.[46]

There seem to have been many reasons for such high levels of alcohol consumption. To begin with, ale was an essential item of diet when water supplies were non-existent or unhealthy; secondly there was a perception that ale or beer was good for strength and health; thirdly there have always been an enormous number of social occasions and rituals bound up with drinking. Finally of course there was the stark fact that for many people drunkenness provided the only real escape from the harsh realities of life.

By the beginning of the First World War non alcoholic drinks were increasingly available and water supplies were more reliable. Consumption of beer reduced to four and a half pints per head and, as has been seen, the First World War marked a turning point in the nation's alcohol consumption.

Changing social and religious attitudes after the war led, amongst other things, to changing attitudes towards drinking. Excessive drinking gradually came to be regarded more as a social than a moral problem, one which had its roots in poor housing, education or working conditions.

The twentieth century saw a continued decline in alcohol consumption but by the beginning of the twenty first century increasing consumption by young people and perceptions of a 'binge drinking culture' have fuelled fears of a return to the 'bad old days'. The moral and nationalistic attitudes of the Victorian and Edwardian era may have been replaced by attitudes based on medico-social issues, but concern about problems associated with excessive drinking is once again high on the national agenda.

Superscript abbreviations   CT Cornish Times

1. Paul Jennings, *The Local: A History of the English Pub*, The History Press, 2011, p.20
2. Peter Haydon, *An Inebriated History of Britain*, Sefton Publishing, 2005, pp. 3-5
3. Haydon, p.8
4. Haydon, p.5, quoting from H V Monckton, *A History of English Ale and Beer*, Bodley Head, 1966 [no page reference given]
5. Nicholas Orme, *Cornwall and the Cross: Christianity 500-1560*, University of London, 2007, pp.113-4
6. Orme, p.56
7. Richard Carew, *The Survey of Cornwall*, Tamar Books, 2004, pp.80-81
8. Carew, p.82
9. See, e.g. L. E. Elliott-Binns, *Medieval Cornwall*, Methuen & Co., London, 1956, p.252
10. Haydon, p.16
11. 5 & 6 Edward VI, c.25
12. David Hey, *The Oxford Companion to Local and Family History*, Oxford University Press, 2002, p.236
13. Calendar of State Papers Domestic, 1577. The hundreds are the western ones of Kerrier, Trigg, Pydar and Powder
14. Carew, p.77
15. John Norden, *A Topographical and Historical Description of Cornwall*, Frank Graham, Newcastle, 1966, p.22
16. James Whetter, *Cornwall in the Seventeenth Century*, Lodeneck press, 1974, pp.8-9
17. Haydon, 2005, p.48
18. Jennings, p.34
19. Jennings, p.37, Brian Vale & Griffith Edwards, *Physician to the Fleet, The Life and Times of Thomas Trotter, 1760-1832*, The Boydell Press, 2010
20. H L Douch, *Old Cornish Inns and Their Place in the Social History of Cornwall*, D Bradford Barton Ltd., 1966, p.25
21. Jennings, p.40
22. Jennings, p.40
23. Jennings, p.52
24. Jennings, p.62
25. Douch, p.104
26. Jennings, p.69
27. Sydney Smith, 1826, quoted in Jennings, p.58
28. Jennings, p.69
29. Haydon, 2008, p.242
30. Parliamentary Papers 1833, [416], p.99, noted in Jennings, p.138
31. County and Borough Police Act, 1856
32. Jennings, p.144
33. Jennings, p.159
34. Haydon, 2008, p.236
35. H Carter, *The Control of the Drinks Trade in Britain. A Contribution to National Efficiency During the Great War 1915-1918*, Longmans, 1919, pp.37-52, quoted in Jennings, p.185
36. Jennings, p.193
37. Jennings, p.193
38. Haydon, p.305
39. Jennings, p.212-213
40. Jennings, p.91
41. Jennings, p.95
42. *Sherborne Mercury* 17th April and Royal Cornwall Gazette, 22nd June 1816
43. Jennings, pp.90-95
44. Jennings, p.117
45. Licensing Act 2003
46. Statistics taken from Jennings, pp.123-124

CHAPTER 2

A Quart of Beer and a Hogshead of Cider

By Alastair Tinto and Nikki Chaplin

Beer

In 1413 a rather troublesome woman called Alice Kelwa was brought before Halton Manor Court in St. Dominick because she "entered the house of William Hoper and took and carried away the bread and beer found there". Beer was a staple of the mediaeval diet and continued to be so well into the nineteenth century. In 1702, when a carpenter called Walter Pomery was on his deathbed, the overseers of the poor paid three shillings for "beer and bread and candlelight". A hundred years later when Ann Mutton, the mother of an illegitimate child, was sent before the magistrates in 1797 for an examination to discover which parish was responsible for her the overseers paid three shillings for "beer and biscuit for shee and her mother".

Whilst excessive drunkenness was frowned upon, beer was a central part of the culture in early modern times. It was regularly drunk at funerals. Indeed, it was regarded as such an essential part of the event that the overseers of the poor in St. Dominick on several occasions even paid for it at paupers' funerals. In 1696, for example, they paid 2s 6d for beer at the funeral of John Hender and a year later 4s 6d for "beer and other things" at John Edgcomb's funeral. Beer was not the only alcohol that was drunk at funerals. In 1772 the overseers contributed one shilling for "a pint of wine for the funeral" of Joan Jane. And a few years later in 1780, when they were "carrying out a survey and selling Marten Congdon's goods" after his death, they paid two shillings "for a pint of gin when the goods was sold".

In St. Dominick beer does not seem to have been as important as cider. Between 1621 and 1749 twenty five inventories refer to cider, ranging from Johane Grubb's hogshead worth seven shillings in 1627 to the 26 hogsheads – 1404 gallons! – of William Geach in 1749.[2] On the other hand in over three hundred wills and many inventories there are no references to beer. This contradicts the conventional view that everyone drank beer. Was the Tamar Valley different from other areas? Or was there something special about St. Dominick? Work needs to be done on other parishes to answer these questions.

The raw material for beer is malted barley, although from time to time other grains were used - in 1631, for instance, Richard Skinnerd, a blacksmith from Baber, had "2½ bushels of oaten malt" worth ten shillings. There is plenty of evidence that barley was grown in this area. Thirty five wills and inventories from St. Dominick between 1603 and 1756 refer to barley, either "in the mow", as was the case for Ezekiel Skinner in 1623, or in the ground, like William Jane's "17 acres barley £25 10s" in his fields at Bohetherick in 1687. Perhaps as much as fifteen percent of the arable land in the seventeenth and eighteenth centuries in St. Dominick was planted with barley. There was a similar amount of oats and the rest was wheat. How much of this barley was used for beer making is hard to tell.[3] In 1631, after the failure of the harvest the year before which had caused much distress in Cornwall, Sir John Trelawney reported that " the price of wheat is att 7d the gallon, Barley at 4d ... and oates att 2d".[4] The poor used barley as their breadcorn because it was cheaper, even though the quality of the bread was not as good. We know that this was sometimes the case in St. Dominick because in 1707 the overseers paid 1s 6d to "Thomas Harris for a peck and half of barley for young Collings wife" who was pregnant with her third child. Barley was also used as animal fodder. So, whilst barley "was primarily a drink cereal",[5] we cannot assume that just because a farmer grew barley he also brewed his own beer. Indeed, although referring to the 1820s, Edwin Jaggard says that in Cornwall only "moderate amounts were destined for the maltsters".[6]

In order to make beer, malt needs to be made from the barley by steeping it in water to get it to germinate and then as soon as the shoots appear drying it in a kiln to stop further growth. Malting barley, which requires careful control of temperature and humidity, is therefore a much more complex process than pressing the juice from apples to get the ingredients for cider. The malt then has to be crushed in a mill and mixed or mashed with water which is boiled with hops or other flavourings before it is fermented. What evidence is there in our records for this complicated brewing process taking place on farms in the way that cider obviously was?

Taking St. Dominick inventories as an example, between 1603 and 1631 there are six references to malt. Tristram Tibb's "20 bushel barley & barley malt" worth £4 in 1629 is typical. However, after 1629 there is no mention of malt in the St. Dominick records other than two malt mills, but these both come about one hundred years later. Richard Doidge, who lived at Westcott, is recorded as having one in 1724 and there was one at Stockwell when Richard Crabb, a tanner, died in 1742. There are only two references to hops. In

1644 Richard Jane of Bohetherick had "hoopes at the Glebe and Calstocke towne" worth 20s and eighty years later in 1722 John Clarke, the lord of the manor at Halton, had "in the Apple Chamber 5 bags hopps".[7]

Clearly, therefore, brewing was taking place in St. Dominick and adjoining areas on a domestic scale at least until the middle of the eighteenth century. None of these people were professional brewers or maltsters: five were farmers or yeomen; there was a tanner, a weaver and a blacksmith; and John Clarke was lord of the manor. We know that generally "beer brewing had undergone a major revolution in the period 1500-1640 and brewing, which had been done in the villages in the Middle Ages, especially by alewives, became an urban occupation".[8] Our evidence suggests that this had happened in St. Dominick. The three houses mentioned in the eighteenth century, Westcott, Stockwell and Halton, were all large properties so it would seem that by about 1650 domestic scale brewing, except in some larger establishments, had more or less come to an end.

Commercial malting and brewing was well established in Cornwall in the early years of the seventeenth century. In 1631 because of the shortage of corn the magistrates in the Hundred of East [East Cornwall] "restraine comon maltsters from makinge barley mault; and endeavoured and still do endeavour to lesson the number of maultmakers, common brewers and tipplers". It is perhaps significant too that the first evidence of public houses in St. Dominick comes in 1633 when "John Rowe and Andrew Elliot paid three shillings a piece towards the use of the poore there for their disorder in an alehouse". Two years later in 1635 George Harris, Ellis Box, John Slade, William Brent and Richard Slade of St. Dominick were "punished for keeping comon selling of ale and beere without license by paying the penalty of XXs. [20 shillings] a piece to the use of the poore of the said parish". There was clearly a thriving drinking culture in St. Dominick. How quaint that these disorderly drinkers and those who supplied them were required to pay for their unruliness by contributing to the poor! It almost makes their offences acceptable.[9]

The inventory taken in 1722 when John Clarke died gives a good idea of the large scale on which brewing at a manor house like Halton Barton took place. He had a malthouse where there were nine casks and a stone cistern. Next to that was a separate brewhouse with a furnace and a couple of brass pans, two corn chests, three casks, three keeves and a keeve horse on which to rest the barrels. Further down the house was a still chamber, where they must have distilled liquor, with one old distiller worth five shillings. Next to that was the apple chamber where amongst other things his hops were kept. John Clarke did not do things by halves!

The earliest commercial brewery of which we have any evidence was in Callington in the 1720s when George Knill, the surgeon, owned a "house and malthouse which Jacob Geach rents and a little meadow which Bartholomew rents and belonging to the malthouse".[10]

It is not until the 1840s that the sources are good enough to tell us much about commercial breweries but by then there were plenty. In June 1842[WB] the fifty six year lease of the *Newport Inn*, Callington, was offered for sale, including a brew-house and an extensive range of equipment. John Bickle was the brewer there, although at the time of the sale he was not the licensee. In 1849 Edward Dingle occupied a "dwelling house and malt house and tenement which he now occupies including the Court and Stables at the back of the Ring O Bells".[11] From at least 1841 up to his death in 1864 Simon Philp was a brewer and maltster in Stoke Climsland, as were William Perkins or Parkin [1841-1851] and a Skinner [1851.] In the 1860s James Rowe combined grocery with brewing[DR] and ran the *Ring O' Bells*. On Cotehele Quay there was a brewery and malthouse behind what is now the *Edgcumbe Arms*. In 1841 John Bickle was maltster. In the same year Nicholas Procter was brewing at Brooklands Farm in Metherell and continued to do so into the 1850s. William Chynoweth had a brewery at Newton in Calstock parish in 1841 and ten years later John Toll, gentleman, was brewer and maltster probably in the same place. A brewery is shown on the Tithe Map in Calstock behind the

This 1808 print from 'Early Trades and Industries' shows a small scale brewing business, which may have been similar to those mentioned above. There is a malting mill on the left and large copper in the centre that the woman is stoking. A mash is being mixed with a large paddle

Naval and Commercial Hotel, and in 1851 John Joll living with John Hutchings at the *Tamar Inn* gave his profession as brewer. In Albaston in the 1851 census there were two breweries, one owned by the Bowhay family and the other by Thomas Read. Ten years later this second brewery was run by William Perkins. The Tamar brewery was beside New Bridge in Gunnislake for a time, probably in the building that later became the Caledonian Hotel. At Halton Quay in St. Dominick from at least the late 1830s there were a malt kiln, some maltsters' cottages and a pub called the *Maltster's Arms* run by Stephen Martin who was also the maltster.[12]

By the 1860s all these little local breweries had disappeared leaving brewing in the Tamar valley to two larger concerns, the Bowhays of Albaston and Thomas "Brewer" Martin of Towell in St. Dominick.

The Bowhays of Albaston were the biggest brewers in the area although. they were also farmers and tanners [DR]. Moreover, not only did they brew beer, they also owned a chain of at least ten public houses which they leased out and which no doubt were required to buy their beer. Their pubs included the *Queen's Head* in Albaston, the *Bull's Head* in Callington, the *Tavistock* and the *Market* in Gunnislake, the *New Inn* in Calstock, the *Maltster's Arms* in Luckett as well as pubs in St. Ann's Chapel, Linkinhorne and Maders.[13]

number of pubs. In 1863 he paid £238 to have assigned to him a mortgage the *Cornish Arms* in St. Dominick, obtaining in the same transaction the leases on four cottages in Churchtown.[16] He never ran the pub, leaving that to his tenant, William Nanscawen Lucas, but it obviously fitted well with the brewing business. He also had properties elsewhere in St. Dominick and in Metherell. In Callington he held the leases for the *Coachmaker's Inn*, *Market Inn* and the *Sun Inn*.[17] When Martin died in 1896 his business was carried on for a short while by his son, Joseph, but when Joseph died in 1903 at the young age of thirty-five the brewery had to close down because there was no-one else to carry on the business.[18] The Bowhays then had the field to themselves. They continued in business, brewing and supplying the pubs of the area, until Thomas Taylor Bowhay retired just before the Second World War.

Bob Martin with a truck loaded with "cyder apples" outside the Cornish Arms, Gunnislake in the 1930s. [Photograph courtesy of Marion Martin via Calstock Archive Trust]

In the 1850s Stephen Martin's son, Thomas, was the brewer at Cotehele in partnership with his brother-in-law George Sargent. Then in 1860 he acquired the one hundred acre farm at Towell in St. Dominick where he quickly set up a "malt house and brew house",[14] which became a thriving business run initially run by Elizabeth, Thomas's wife. In 1861 she employed five men in the brewery.

Known for most of his life as "Brewer Martin", Thomas was a larger than life figure. Doris Webber, his great-niece, described him as "very rich" and said that he "considered himself rather superior to us".[15] Like the Bowhays, Martin held the leases of a

Cider

Cider was an everyday drink for the farmers of East Cornwall from mediaeval times onwards. Fruit trees grow well in this area, and looking at land records from Calstock parish in the 1700s, it is clear that most holdings included an acre or two of orchard. Cider was less dangerous to drink than the unreliable water sources and the religious houses, such as the monks at Tavistock Abbey set the example: in 1475, for instance, cider processed at the Abbots cider press at Plymstock was shipped up the Tamar and unloaded at Morwellham.[19] Often the apples had previously been sent down from this area to Plymstock for processing.

Cidermaking seems to have been widespread in the Tamar Valley: the reeve of Halton manor sent cider to Trematon castle, "and allowed to the reeve of the same 6s 10d for a pipe of cider bought for Trematon castle for food etc. Item, in carriage of the same pipe 12d".[20]

Kneebone noted in 1684 that in the hundred of East [East Cornwall] "there is throughout the whole abundance of profitable Orchards whence syder as good as any unmixt elsewhere in the land is produced".[21] Cider, very likely to be from the Tamar Valley, was bought by victuallers in Elizabethan times for the provisioning of ships.[22] At harvest time, cider was included in the wages of part-time labourers right up until the twentieth century.

Cider was clearly made on many farms. The probate inventory for Marke Martyn, junior, dated 1st April 1624, and living in Calstock parish, includes "cyder valued at 2s; 3 laders at 2s; hogsheads, and other tymber vessell at 58s". Ladders were essential for collecting tree fruit, and the fact that he had so many barrels indicates that he may well have been producing a large amount of cider. Elizabeth Tibb's inventory in 1669, records "one pound to make cider with & all the tacle thereunto belonging £1 2s 6d". Hers is one of fourteen St. Dominick wills and inventories to refer to apples mills or cider pounds.

The value of the cider varies from 4s for a hogshead and a half of "sider"[23] to more than a pound each – 15 hogsheads of syder valued at £16 2s 6d [Inventory of Richard Bligh, Calstock parish, 22nd February 1713].[24] The wooden hogs-heads, keeves and barrels were of value without cider in them – Thomas Jagoe of Calstock had 3 hogsheads, 2 keeves and wooden vessel valued at 10s, out of a total inventory of £14 6s 8d.[25] The cider pound was even more valuable - one pound for apples with its furniture was valued at £3 in the 1664 inventory of Henry Aunger, Yeoman, of St. Dominick.[26] Apples were valued separately, in the will of Mary Pearse [widow], Calstock parish, dated 28th Jan 1618 "her apples in the house - 1s",[27] The will of Agnes Stephen [widow] Calstock parish dated 5th February 1620 shows "½ a bushell of apples - 6d".[28] James

Adam's inventory of 1602 includes apples valued at 20s, which would have been twenty bushels [or half a ton] at the rate that Agnes Stephen's apples were valued. If a bushel makes about three gallons of cider, his crop would have produced sixty gallons.

In 1622, James Gadgecombe of St. Dominick left his father "all my syder". In 1679 Prudence Horrill, a widow, left "my tenant Nicholas Symons £3 and the cider which is in his hogshead". In 1731, in making provision in his will for his wife, Michael Fletcher instructed his executors to ensure that "twelve quart bottles are to be filled every year with good cyder and apples for her own use when they are in the garden and 1 bushel every year for her Hord of what sort she will".

Landowners required their tenants to take care of the orchards. The 1767 lease for Heathfield in St. Dominick instructed the tenant "to replace apple trees wanting" on pain of forfeiting ten shillings for each tree. In April 1769 the sale of Hampt, Luckett included "pound houses, apple chambers, a large number of orchards in prime and others not long since planted with the best cyder fruit trees".[SM] Two years later, in May 1771, Hampt was again advertised to let, with an orchard which usually produced "100 hogsheads of cider per year",[SM] a considerable amount; and even at a moderate price

Apple harvesting in orchards at Bittams
Photograph courtesy of the Calstock Archive Trust

of ten shillings per hogshead, it would have been worth £50. Land at Latchley and Chilsworthy was described in the 'West Briton' on 16th August 1850, "The orchards are very productive and in their prime. The cider made on this estate is much sought after; the fruit being of the first quality, the late proprietor always commanded his own prices".

Robert Fraser carried out a survey of Devon and Cornwall in 1794 for the Board of Agriculture. "Cider constitutes a very material article of rural economy. Every farmer has his orchard, which supplies him, in the first place, with an agreeable and wholesome beverage for himself and family, and the surplus he disposes of to the cider merchant". His report included details of apple production and varieties, and noted that farm labourers "wages are 1s a day and a quart of cyder. In harvest wages much the same with as much cyder as they chuse to drink".[29]

G.B. Worgan was impressed by Cornwall's orchards in his survey of agriculture in Cornwall for the Board of Agriculture in 1811.[30] The Tamar Valley got a special mention in Lysons Magna Britannica in 1814: "Orchards abound in all the southern parts of the county, in some parts of Stratton and in that part of the hundred of East which borders on the Tamar particularly in the parishes of Calstock, Stoke Climsland, St. Dominick and Landulph. The best cyder made in this district is from an apple called the Duffling which is a rich and strong-bodied liquor.... But it is not made in large quantities and only for home consumption".

James Lawry, the Victorian horticulturalist who developed the strawberry industry in the Tamar Valley wrote of "orchards first planted in Queen Elizabeth's time," naming Gilliflower and Sops in Wine as popular varieties.[31] There were countless local varieties of apples; some only grown within a parish and others used across the area. Some were favoured for cider making, but often farmers would use whatever was to hand for their brew.

Cider for farm workers and labourers continued into the twentieth century as the drink of choice, rather than beer. Fred Collins recalled that at some farms in the 1930s "they'd have a barrel of scrumpy" for the threshing machinists[32] and Peter Langsford remembered around the same time that at Halton Quay when they were unloading coal from the barges that came up from Plymouth "Jimmy Bowden and Coffin Lane kept going on cider, sweating and winching [the coal] up by hand".[33]

Cider-making continued to be widespread in East Cornwall villages until the 1970s, and the process hasn't changed for hundreds of years. In some cases the presses, particularly the beam presses, were ancient. Screw presses were also used. The beam press used by the Pridham family of Prospect Farm in Latchley was thought to be three hundred years old in the mid-twentieth century. "There'd be calves in the pound house until cider making time. There was a granite trough. The dung had to be forked out first, and the trough was swilled out. Children used to push the apples down a little hole, there'd be a crusher below that, with four men turning the handles. Then apples would be shovelled from there across to the vat. Then they'd make what they called the cheese, a layer of apples, a layer of straw and so on. Then a slab of wood, called the sow, went on top of that, and then there was the boar, another piece of timber, on top of that. Then the press would come down and squeeze the apple juice into the trough, dipped out from there into the barrels and allowed to ferment until it stopped". [Roger Pridham][34]

With the beam press, the weight of the stone pressed on the 'cheese' overnight, squeezing out the juice. The next evening the cider makers would lift the stone back up to the top and let it drop to squeeze the apples again; and so it went on until the juice stopped running. A screw press needed regular attention to tighten the screw and squeeze the apples.

Beam press at Cotehele House
[Photograph courtesy of Calstock Archive Trust]

"Us wouldn't throw away no days like in making cider. Hup the stones up, well up on the cheese, evenings. That was our job. To pare it, put un up again. You know, when you press it back, put the stones, throw them up. That from the ground, two great stones, must be 'bout twelve hundred weight apiece... Then they got all the next day to do down. Then when they's down, in the evening again, let it back a bit, then 'eave it up and pare un again". [Gerald Pridham][35]

Superscript abbreviations
SM   Sherborne and Yeovil Mercury
WB   West Briton
DR   Street or Postal Directory

1.   Halton Manor Court Rolls, 24th September 1413, National Archive, SC2.159/27
2.   A hogshead of ale was 54 gallons or 240 litres
3.   This is an estimate on the amounts of the various grains mentioned in St. Dominick inventories between 1603 and 1756
4.   Certificates of Justices of the Peace, 1st May 1631, National Archive, SP/16/190/2
5.   Joan Thirsk editor, *The Agrarian History of England and Wales, Vol.IV* 1500-1640, Cambridge University Press, 1967, p.627
6.   Edwin Jaggard, *Cornwall Politics in the Age of Reform 1790-1885*, The Royal Historical Society, Woodbridge Suffolk, 1999, p.40
7.   Wills and Inventories, available at the Cornwall Record Office
8.   Thirsk, p.334
9.   Certificates of Justices of the Peace, 6th May 1631, SP/16/190/37 and 8th May 1633, SP16/284/61
10. Inventory of George Knill, 1738, Cornwall Record Office, AP/K/745
11. Alison Highet, *The Dingle Family*, July 2008, Callington Heritage Centre Newsletter, p.4
12. St. Dominick Highway Rate, Cornwall Record Office, DDP/50/20/1, 1841 census, Churchwardens Accounts, CRO, DDP/50/5
13. Bowhay Account Book, Calstock Parish Archive
14. St. Dominick Select Vestry Minutes, 11th April 1861, CRO, DDP/50/8/1
15. Natalie Allen, *A Stitch in Time*, N. R. Allen, Saltash, 1984 p.77
16. Indenture, Transfer of Mortgage on Cornish Arms from Samuel Lang and William and Robert Lucas to Thomas Martin, CRO
17. Register of Licences, 1872-1893, CRO, JC/EMID/26
18. Allen, p.15
19. H P R Finberg, *Tavistock Abbey. A Study in the Social and Economic History of Devon*, David & Charles, 1969
20. Account Roll for Henry IV, 1405/6, Robert W Dunning [ed.] *The Hylle Cartulary*, Somerset Record Society, Vol.LXVIII, Frome, 1968, no.229
21. Edward Kneebone, *Hundred of the East*, British Museum, Add MSS 334.20
22. W G Hoskins, *Devon*, Collins, 1954
23. Calstock Parish Archive, Ref.3251
24. Inventory of Richard Bligh 1713, Calstock Parish Archive, Ref. 4216
25. Thomas Jagoe inventory, 3rd September 1618, Calstock Parish Archive, Ref. 2122
26. Inventory of Henry Aunger, 1664, mentioned in Douch
27. Will of Mary Pearse, Calstock Parish Archive, Ref.2134
28. Will of Agnes Stephen, 1620, Calstock Parish Archive
29. Robert Fraser, *General View of the County of Cornwall* and *General View of Agriculture of Devon*, 1794, reprinted Porcupine Barnstaple 1970
30. G B Worgan, *General View of the Agriculture of Cornwall*, B McMillan, 1811
31. Collins Cornwall, publisher Collins 1893 quoting Journal of the Royal Agricultural Society, 1892
32. Allen, p.63
33. Transcript of taped interview with Mr. Peter Langsford at Calstock Parish Archive
34. Transcript of taped interview with Mr. Roger Pridham at Calstock Parish Archive
35. Transcript of taped interview with Mr. Gerald Pridham at Calstock Parish Archive

CHAPTER 3

The Sober Alternative

By Lynda Mudle-Small

As we have seen in Chapter 1, from before mediaeval times, alcohol was part of everyday life as there was little else to drink. Even in the countryside the sources of pure, unpolluted water were scarce. It was much safer to drink beer or cider that had been through a boiling or fermentation process. In the eighteenth and early nineteenth centuries many rural homes and farms would brew their own beer or cider. In towns it was common, on a daily basis, for someone to go a few yards to their nearest alehouse, for a jug of beer for the house.

In the many farms throughout the county, home brewed beer or cider was thought essential to hospitality, health and good relations with servants. Agricultural workers long believed it was impossible to get in the harvest without harvest beer, or in the West Country, cider.

The life of the working classes was one long hard toil and there were few comforts available. Houses were often damp, with bare earth floors and the absolute minimum of furniture. It is therefore not surprising that the warmth of the local hostelry was sought by many working men, especially the single man.

George Sims, an advocate of the temperance movement, wrote about the appalling living conditions that drove the poor to drink. He considered that: "drink gives them the Dutch courage necessary to go on living; drink dulls their senses and reduces them to the level of the brutes they must be to live in such places".[1]

Until the nineteenth century there were no real alternatives to alcoholic drinks and during the first decades of the nineteenth century the price of alcohol was steadily dropping. Gin, the scourge of the late eighteenth century, became even cheaper in the 1820s. In Cornwall in June 1822 the price of beer dropped from 3d to 2d a quart and only two years later the cost of a publican's spirit licence was reduced from £5 to £2 if his house was under a ratable value of £10 p.a.[2] However, the main contributory factor to the ready availability of alcohol in the early Victorian era was the Beer Act of 1830, which not only made the setting up of beer shops very easy but completely removed the tax on beer and cider.

In Cornwall this coincided with the mining boom and a greater mobility of the working class who moved from mine to mine seeking work. Many miners were single men who found the beer shop a warm and comfortable retreat from the long hours of manual labour, often in appalling conditions. Unlike earlier drinking places, beer shops catered for only the poorest type of labourer. They often resembled cottages rather than public-houses, with just a licence board above the door. With the ease in obtaining a licence the population were not slow at meeting the need. Beer shops sprung up everywhere, often run by miner's wives or widows, who used the sale of beer to supplement their incomes. Invariably discord followed, the 'Royal Cornwall Gazette' reporting in January 1835 that "the riotous conduct of the profligate frequenters of those pests of the Mining districts, the beer shops, has risen to so alarming a pitch, that for the preservation of the peace of some districts, and for the protection of the reputable part of the population, it has become absolutely necessary to swear in most of the Mine Agents as special constables".

Whilst the miners kept to themselves and their shanty towns on the moors, away from the long-standing residents, it was not too bad, but when gangs of miners descended on villages and towns, the impact on the law-abiding respectable citizens was profound.

Hamilton Jenkins[3] mentions that:- "On Saturday nights after pay-day, the populous villages of Caradon Town, Pensilva, Minions and Crows Nest were crowded with men, and resembled in character the mining camps of Colorado and the Far West". If it was like this in the villages on the south-east edge of Bodmin Moor, it must have been much the same in all the mining villages from the Moor to the River Tamar.

On Saturday 7th May 1842, when a large group of miners in the *Buller's Arms* in Liskeard were refused more drink, a riot ensued. When the ringleaders were taken into custody over two hundred miners stormed the house and rescued them and kept the inhabitants of the town "in a state of fear and tumult until six the next morning".[WB]

Virtually all towns and villages within proximity of mines suffered and it is not difficult to imagine what the respectable residents thought about the changes in society that were blamed on the miners, alcohol and drunkenness. It was not just mining villages and towns that suffered. In October 1851 in East Looe, twelve new constables were sworn in "to suppress all vice and disorderly conduct committed by the assembling of young men in the streets at night, thereby insulting and obstructing persons passing by, and in various ways annoying the public".[WB] In April 1859 the complaints continued with a letter to the editor of the 'Cornish Times' about Gunnislake where "groups of men and boys are allowed to stand in the streets on Sundays to the annoyance of the people at the Chapels. At the place where I attend stones were thrown in at the door on Sunday last, and the congregation disturbed by very unpleasant noises".

One of the many temperance posters produced nationally.
This one is circa 1830

The Temperance Movement
Arrives in Cornwall

Organized religion has attacked drunkenness and excess at least since Anglo Saxon times, but total abstinence from alcohol was very rarely advocated or practiced. In society as it was, at beginning of the nineteenth century, alcohol was a formidable antagonist for any reformer to take on.

The temperance movement, which was originally non-religious, started as an anti-spirit campaign in Scotland and Ireland which arrived in England in 1830. However it is Joseph Livesey, a politician and newspaper owner in Preston, who is credited with starting the temperance movement in 1832. He was the author of *The Pledge,* which he required followers to sign:

> *"We agree to abstain from all liquors*
> *of an intoxicating quality whether ale,*
> *porter, wine or ardent spirits, except*
> *as medicine, and to observe great*
> *moderation in the use of fermented*
> *liquors, such as wine, beer, cider,*
> *etc".*

Note that this is a temperance pledge as opposed to a total abstinence pledge, although the word temperance and teetotal are frequently confused.

It did not take long for the movement to reach Cornwall. In April 1832[WB] there was the inaugural meeting of the Temperance Society in Truro, when the chair was taken by a Baptist Minister, and forty-one intending members subscribed to the pledge.

In November 1837 it was reported that temperance societies, "since the introduction of the pledge of total abstinence from all intoxicating drinks, have made rapid progress.......The eastern part of our own county has joined the movement. At Launceston, a public meeting was held on the 15th instant; and is to be followed by public discussions, which commenced on the 21st in the British School-room".[4]

A Temperance Society was formed in Liskeard on 12th December 1837[5] after a lecture by Dr Henry Mudge from Bodmin. Callington's Temperance Society held its inaugural meeting in May or June 1839. The 'West Briton' reported on their first anniversary meeting where, unusually for the time, the Anglican minister of St. Dominick, Rev. F L Bazeley, preached the sermon. Then "the members walked in procession through the town, preceded by banners and a band of music". The well-patronized assembly rooms at Golding's Hotel were not used for the tea that followed [the Goldings were also Spirit and Wine Merchants], but the loan of the market place was accepted. At this meeting about forty signed the pledge.

As may be imagined, the temperance message spread rapidly, especially in mining districts like Callington, Calstock and Caradon where the local inhabitants may have seen it as a remedy for their problems. We know from newspapers that meetings and rallies were widespread, but some were more active in taking the message to the mines. In May 1838 [GAZ] it was claimed that "the total abstinence principle continues to work wonders in the west. It runs from the towns into the villages and hamlets, like wildfire, pursuing the drunkard even into his most obscure haunts". Nearly ten years later in 1847 there was another motivation to temperance as the price of corn was so high that hunger and starvation haunted the poor. There were food riots throughout the county. In May, two hundred miners descended on Callington, forcing farmers to sell their corn and butter at a reasonable price. "On Saturday evening, a meeting of miners was held in the town hall, when more than two hundred agreed to drink no liquor in any of the Callington public houses, and the first who broke this agreement should be horsed around the town on a pole".[WB]

Even twenty years later individual door-to-door activity was still obtaining recruits in mining villages. In Calstock it was reported in November 1858 that "Mr. Horswell the indefatigable advocate of sobriety and agent of Devonport and Stonehouse Temperance Society by kind permission of the [Temperance] Committee has during the last week been paying house to house visits in Calstock and Morwellham and has also held public meetings. The result of this effort has been the obtaining of three hundred and fifty signatures to the temperance pledge". CT

Meetings continued to be held and each little village eventually formed its own temperance society. In March 1857 sixteen habitual drunkards signed the pledge at a meeting in the Primitive Methodist Chapel in Henwood.CT The momentum continued with Teetotal Societies being formed in Caradon and Rilla Mill in December 1863 where nearly five hundred pledges were made.CT St. Ive [Pensilva] had its own temperance society, the first meeting being held there in 1839 in "a barn fitted up for the occasion, which was crowded".[6]

Temperance concerns were evident in St. Dominick in 1856 when the constables were asked "to make an arrangement for visiting the public houses more frequently than heretofore especially during the hours of Divine Service and also from time to time report to the Vestry the number of times the public houses have been visited and the state in which they were found to be". The effect of the temperance movement on drinking is less clear. In 1856 the village had a record number of public houses. In 1857 when the *Tamar Inn* was prosecuted the Vestry was divided: "8 hands were held up in favour of the prosecution and 5 against it".[7]

Latchley Band of Hope marching through the village, circa 1900. Photograph courtesy of Calstock Archive Trust

From early in the movement the newspapers came out in support of temperance, championing the teetotallers and condemning reports of drunkenness and disorderly behaviour. Newspaper support from the 'West Briton', 'Royal Cornwall Gazette' and the 'Cornish Times' continued for many decades.

Bands of Hope

As the temperance movement gathered pace it was natural that an organisation was created for younger members. In 1847 the term Band of Hope was first applied to groups of children organized for temperance work and in 1855 a national organisation was formed. Children were encouraged, through Sunday Schools, to influence their parents, if possible, although the reverse is also known, where parents signed up their children. Gunnislake was one of the first villages in the area to form a Band of Hope in 1856.

The Rechabites

The Independent Order of Rechabites was a Friendly Society founded in England in 1835 as part of the temperance movement. Always well connected in upper society and involved in financial matters, it gradually transformed into a financial institution which still exists, and still promotes abstinence. By 1868 it boasted thirteen thousand adult members, and it was during the 1860s that the Order expanded rapidly.

In June 1841 WB "The Rechabites, by the insignia of their order, added much to the interest of the day" at the annual total abstinence festival in St. Austell, where Mr. James Teare "the esteemed and successful advocate of the total abstinence cause" preached. In January 1842WB the Padstow branch of Rechabites claimed that fifty percent of the town, amounting to eleven hundred persons, were now teetotallers. In May 1845 in Bodmin "the meeting was all such as to indicate increasing prosperity, in this, the first working teetotal society in Cornwall". They claimed six hundred members. The Callington Rechabite branch had been formed early in 1841, although in September 1842 WB, when there was a court case involving the funds, "it had not been enrolled".

Opposition & Conflict

Despite the zeal of the new movement there were many opposed to it and there were also conflicts within the movement itself. As we have seen above, alcohol was considered an integral part of normal life and by many it was considered that life itself could not continue without it. For the clergy and the landed gentry it was impossible to consider entertaining without it and they had no intention of giving up their wine, port, brandy and other intoxicants. The medical profession strongly resented the laymen interfering by suggesting that alcohol should not be used as a medicine, Dr H Mudge of Bodmin being one of the few early exceptions.

In the first half of the nineteenth century many of the early leaders of the temperance movement were prominent business men and traders rather than churchmen. Less than fourteen percent of the leaders of the temperance movement were Anglicans[8]; this is what made the sermon by the Rev. F L Bazeley of St. Dominic in 1840 so unusual.

Initially there were conflicts between the temperance and teetotal groups; definitions of the meaning of the two words is unclear even to this day. Both can mean abstinence, although temperance can also mean moderation. The lack of clarity between the two words is also evident in newspaper quotations. As we have seen a Temperance Society was formed in Truro in 1832 and a Teetotal Association had its inaugural meeting in Truro in September 1838[9]. When James Teare a teetotal missionary from Preston, toured Cornwall in 1837/38, "his effect was instantaneous and his impact enormous". A thousand people attended his first meeting at St. Austel.[10]. One of the locations he attended was St. Agnes. A 'Cornwall Gazette' correspondent commented that; "Mr. Teare is very successful in winning the approbation of those who hear him, especially among the working classes; but in some instances, his remarks are rather intemperate, especially towards the Temperance Society, which is every whit as respectable as his own, and perhaps stands on a more lasting foundation".

Teetotalism was stronger amongst the non-conformists, especially the offshoots such as the Primitive Methodists and the Bible Christians. It was also strongly championed by the Quakers. Initially the Wesleyan Methodists turned their back on temperance and shut the doors of their chapels to such meetings, following a motion at the 1841 Conference. However the official Wesleyan condemnation of teetotalism was never unanimously accepted within the denomination in Cornwall, and many teetotallers fought battles in the 1840s for entry into their chapels. In 1891 historians of the temperance movement said that "From 1841 to 1850 the other branches of the Methodist family had to succor and support the persecuted and afflicted teetotallers of Cornwall".[11] So enthusiastic for teetotalism were many Cornish Wesleyans that they defied the conference. There are many examples of this in newspapers. In Callington in 1844 [WB] the fifth anniversary of the teetotal association listened to a sermon in "a chapel belonging to the Wesleyan Association".

Opposition did not just come from part of the religious sector; there were attacks from other interests. The temperance movement faced abuse from those with a vested interest in the alcohol trade, not just the beer shop keepers and publicans but the stronger brewery interests as well as all their hard-core drinking customers.

In Liskeard in 1838[WB] a drunken anti-temperance mob smashed the windows of the hall in which a temperance meeting was taking place. In St. Agnes in 1842 [WB] the Vestry carried a motion that no teetotaller should be eligible for the office of parish constable. And in 1851[WB] a train from St. Austell taking a teetotal anniversary outing to the Cheesewring could easily have been derailed had not someone spotted that a "portion of the rail [had been] feloniously removed by some individual unknown".

In 1843 and June 1844 huge rallies were convened at Roughtor where thousands of temperance supporters attended, [Ten thousand attendance claimed in 1844]. After the first festival the local publicans and anti-temperance protesters spotted an opportunity to promote their interests and set up alternative 'rowdy' activities such as donkey racing and wrestling, "the consequence of this was, that the well-disposed were interrupted, and there was a great deal of drunkenness".[WB] Whilst the orderly part of the company listened to addresses and sermons; "The standings and refreshment booths were very numerous, and most of them appeared busily employed". The drunken revelry continued until very late, long after the temperance supporters had left.

Despite the efforts of the temperance movement to prove that farming and especially harvesting, could be executed without the use of alcohol, the production of cider on farms continued for many decades. Agricultural labourers considered it to be part of their wage and as farmers did not want to pay more in lieu of cider, the practice continued. Hogsheads of surplus cider [54 gallons/240 litres] were regularly being advertised for sale in local newspapers.

Non-Alcoholic Drinks

At the same time as the temperance campaigners were trying to rid the country of alcohol, they were indirectly assisted by the advance in the provision of non-alcoholic drinks. Although the movement as a whole had no policy on the provision of alternative drinks, by their use it supported them at its meetings, especially tea. Where the societies as a whole failed, individual prominent teetotallers were often responsible for the promotion and distribution of alternative drinks, and in providing the facilities within which to enjoy them.

Water

As already mentioned, many sources of water were not pure enough to be used as drinking water. In 1849 there were serious outbreaks of cholera in all the main towns of Cornwall. In Callington over half the population succumbed to the disease and the 'West Briton' recorded over seventy deaths. It was not until Dr Snow discovered, in 1854, that this was a water-borne disease that serious consideration was given to the water supplies. Although schemes for the provision of clean water to major cities were drawn up, it was not until the 1870s that water could be considered safe to drink and it was even later than this in the rural towns and villages. Although Callington had been part of a Rural Sanitary Authority, which was established in 1873, in 1885 Dr D S Davies, when reporting to the Local Government Board, stated that along the supply of water to Pipe Well, there were "great possibilities of harm should specific contaminants gain access to the supply". It was not until 1886 when Callington Water Company was formed that a pure water supply was available to residents, although in 1892 it was reported there were still numerous private pumps which were liable to be polluted.[12]

Carbonated Drinks

J. J. Schweppe's carbonated mineral water and lemonades became available on the streets of London in the early 1800s. Ultimately carbonated water changed the way people drank. Instead of drinking spirits neat, soda water and later carbonated soft drinks helped dilute alcohol, mitigating its harsh effects. Brewed ginger beer [non-alcoholic] also became popular.

The Great Exhibition of 1851 was influential in spreading the popularity of non-alcoholic drinks. Many Cornishmen travelled to the capital for the very first time using the new railway. Intoxicants were excluded from the Crystal Palace. "The heat was oppressive throughout the day, and the various fountains were almost drained of their contents by the thirsty visitors".[WB] Over one million bottles of Schweppes soda-water, lemonade and ginger-beer were sold.[13]

The earliest manufacture of non-alcoholic cordials in Cornwall may have been in the 1830s. We know that Messrs. Jenkins and Co., of Truro, were back in production in May 1842[WB] as they had "repaired the damage occasioned by the bursting of their condensing cylinder, and are again able to supply the public with these refreshing summer beverages, in the manufacture of which they have arrived at so high a degree of excellence". More locally, T S Eyre of the Devon and Cornwall Soda Water Manufactory in Launceston was advertising his soda water,

lemonade and gingerade as a summer beverage in April 1859[CT]. The 1850 Directory for Devon shows four 'Ginger, Beer, &c. Mfrs' in Plymouth. There were several mineral water manufacturers in Callington advertising in local directories from the early 1880s although some were probably established in the mid 1870s. John Skinner of the *Commercial Inn* in Calstock was selling ginger beer in his own stoneware bottles around 1880. One ginger beer bottle from W Uglow of Callington appears to date from the 1850s but no records have been found of this manufacturer.[14]

Tea

Tea was introduced for the first time in British society in 1662 by Catherine of Braganza upon her marriage to Charles II. The new trend was soon adopted and the act of drinking tea quickly spread throughout the English bourgeoisie. However tea was heavily taxed and by the mid eighteenth century tax had reached 119%. This created a new industry – tea smuggling. It also led to the adulteration of tea with substances such as willow, licorice, and sloe leaves. Finally, in 1784 William Pitt the Younger introduced the Commutation Act, which dropped the tax on tea from 119% to 12.5%, effectively ending smuggling. Adulteration remained a problem though until the Food and Drug Act of

An advertisement for local non-alcoholic drinks. From Venning's Directory of 1881

1875 brought in stiff penalties to eliminate the practice.[15]

However as with all innovations, there was initially considerable debate about whether tea was good for you. Even John Wesley, the founder of the Methodist movement, entered the debate in 1748 arguing for complete abstinence from tea, on the grounds that it gave rise to "numberless disorders, particularly those of a nervous kind". Wesley urged that the money previously spent by an individual on tea should instead be given to the poor as an alternative hot infusion could be made from English herbs including sage or mint. His argument was certainly thorough [although medically incorrect], and he even touched on how one ought to deal with the awkward situation of having to refuse an offered cup of tea. The tract is shot through with the emphasis on the religious importance of self-denial that was a central tenet of early Methodism, although later in his life Wesley went back to tea drinking.[16]

Throughout the first half of the nineteenth century the price of tea continued to drop with the spread of tea growing to India and the introduction of fast tea clippers to transport it. It gradually came within the reach of the working class and by the 1840s there was little difference in the price of a cup of tea at 2d. and a pot of beer at 3d.

In the east of Cornwall, tea dealers are first mentioned in Pigot & Co.'s Directory of 1844 when, out of seventy five shopkeepers and traders in Callington, there are six tea dealers. Not uncommon at the time were travelling tea dealers and David Kirk and John Vosper plied their tea in the area. However it would seem there was a degree of protectionism and perhaps price fixing. Two interesting court cases reported in January and August 1840[WB] refer to Mr. John Milroy, tea dealer of Callington. William McGuffin, 21, was an employee of John Milroy hired "to carry round tea for sale, and to receive the money. Witness paid him yearly wages; or rather he was to have so much at the end of his time. He had particular rounds every day, and was out two nights in a fortnight". However what had "excited considerable interest, was the facts elicited as to the mode in which they carried on their trade". Mr. Milroy admitting that tea dealers had a rule amongst themselves that they would not deal with any wholesale house that supplies tea to any person interfering with their rounds. In August Mr. Milroy brought another case against William McGuffin who had by then set up for himself as a tea-dealer in Okehampton. The action was brought on a bond by which the defendant engaged, under the penalty of £1,000, not to carry on business as a tea-dealer, within twenty-five miles of Callington. It was proven that McGuffin had broken the bond, but he was only fined forty shillings by the Magistrates. John Cassell, of Fenchurch Street, London, a

pioneering teetotal advocate, vigorously promoted tea from the 1840s and in November 1859[CT] was advertising Mr. E Philp as his Callington agent. His advertisements featured his 'Pure Four Shilling Tea' which was sold in packets from 2oz to 1lb. Throughout the rest of the century the price of tea continued to drop, which was reflected in the increased consumption. The temperance movement promoted tea as the sober alternative at functions.

Coffee

Largely through the efforts of the British East India Company and the Dutch East India Company, coffee became available in England towards the end of the sixteenth century and by 1652 the first coffee house was opened in London. A decision made by the East India Company to concentrate on importing tea instead of coffee led to the demise of the coffee house at this time. But for that decision, coffee could have been the UK's national drink.

A tax deduction in 1808 brought the price of coffee down and in London by the 1840s coffee was cheaper than tea or cocoa and rivalled beer:-

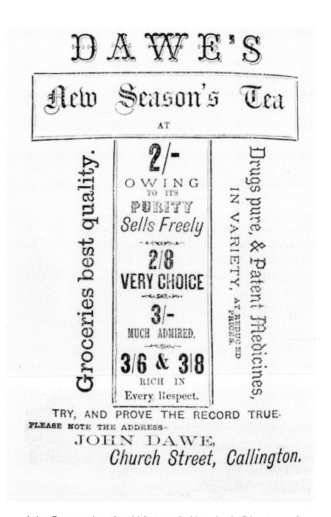

John Dawe advertised his teas in Venning's Directory of 1881. This can be compared with the 'Pure Four Shilling Tea' Mr. Philp stocked in 1859.

Coffee	1½d a cup
Tea	2d a cup
Cocoa	4d a cup
Porter	2½d a pint[17]

In the latter part of the century the temperance movement tried to revive the coffee house scene in an attempt to divert the working man from the perils of drink. Modelled on the mahogany-trimmed taverns promoted by the beer industry, coffee taverns were publicised to show there were beverages as comforting as beer, and as cheap as beer.

In his 1859 advertisement mentioned above, John Cassell was also seeking agents for his coffee. By 1873[DR] Callington had two coffee taverns, one run by the Misses Caroline and Florence Batten and their father, and another by Richard Croker. By 1883[DR] the Misses Batten must have decided that 'coffee rooms' was too prescriptive and had changed the description to 'refreshment rooms'

Cocoa

The original cocoa which arrived in Europe in the sixteenth century was spicy and bitter and was an acquired taste. It was not until cocoa powder was invented in 1838 that it started to become more widely used. It was being promoted in London in the 1840s and reached the rural areas after this. It never rivalled tea or coffee as a daily drink.

Milk

Even in the countryside, milk was not widely considered as a beverage. In urban areas the quality was very dubious. It was not until 1863 that Louis Pasteur invented pasteurization, a method of killing harmful bacteria in food, but it was years

PUBLIC HALL AND COFFEE TAVERN, CALLINGTON.

The Public Hall, Temperance Hotel and Coffee Tavern in Well Street erected in 1885. This sketch is from Venning's Directory of 1901. Currently [2011] this is the Social Club and the coffee tavern is now a corner shop with a locksmith and shoe repair business.

before it became common practice. The dietary value of milk was not recognized at the time, and townsmen bought it less as a beverage in its own right than for making tea, coffee and milk puddings.

Temperance Hotels

Coffee houses have been mentioned as an alternative place in which to meet socially and drink non-alcoholic drinks. From the 1880s refreshment rooms feature in both Callington and Calstock[DR] and there was even a tea shop in Stokeclimsland.[CS] The temperance movement also promoted temperance halls and hotels for their larger meetings rather than patronise establishments that sold alcohol. In Callington the assembly rooms in *Golding's Hotel* had no temperance competition until the Public Hall and Temperance Hotel was erected in Well Street in 1885, a group of prominent teetotallers being instrumental in its construction. Innkeepers could rely on substantial profits from selling intoxicants, whereas temperance hoteliers had no such resource and depended on a limited clientele. Many were speculative ventures, but a few, such as Chubb's Temperance Hotel on the Saltash Road, succeeded well into the twentieth century.

A Religious Movement

Although temperance did not begin as a religious movement it gradually became part of church organizations and by the 1870s had acquired a distinct Christian flavour. The number of abstaining Anglican ministers slowly increased to equal non-conformist ministers and in 1862 the Church of England Temperance Movement was formed. After Archbishop Manning committed himself to the prohibitionist movement in 1868 it became uncommon for religious leaders to oppose temperance movements.[18] Although many individual Wesleyan Methodists were prominent in the movement, the Wesleyans were amongst the last to form their own denominational temperance society. Charles Booth discussing temperance societies in 1890, claimed that they were "almost all connected with some Christian church or mission, and there are few churches or missions which do not interest themselves in this kind of work".[19]

In East Cornwall the movement continued to expand and the activities were regularly reported in the local newspapers. In the 1870s the Church of England Temperance Societies start to feature with Harrowbarrow, Calstock, and Gunnislake being mentioned, as well as Callington and the smaller villages such as Pensilva in St. Ive.

Bands of Hope continued to expand and every village with a church or chapel must have had one. If they had a Sunday School, they would have had a

Band of Hope. Calstock was well represented with long-standing groups in Harrowbarrow and Gunnislake and newer groups in Chilsworthy and Latchley. The Latchley Band of Hope was established in 1882 at the same time as Cross [Monks Cross]. Quethiock held a Band of Hope festival with brass bands, marches, tea and an open air evening meeting.[20] Pensilva had their Band of Hope and there was also one at St. Ive. Golberdon had a group as did Bray Shop and Luckett. Callington had several groups.

New temperance societies continued to be formed. In February 1883 twenty five signed the pledge at the Wesleyan Chapel in Stoke Climsland after a visit from the Callington Total Abstinence Society.[CT] In March of the same year there was a report in the 'Cornish Times' that the "Rilla Mill Teetotal and Band of Hope Society now numbers over 200 members, including the majority of young persons in the village and neighbourhood".

St. Dominick was unusual in that by 1878 it had a Temperance Reading Room and Library[DR]. A Membership Book for 1898-1899 lists fifty-five men [no women] as members.[21] The building continued in use until at least 1920 with Les Babb remembering that a lot of the older men used to go to the "Reading Room by the churchyard" where they would play bagatelle and billiards.[22] It was also referred to as a reading room in 1917 when Bill Stephens was paid for sweeping the chimney.[23]

To illustrate the profusion of temperance and teetotal groups, by 1883 Callington had four different groups: the Callington Total Abstinence Society; the Callington Temperance Society; the United Temperance Society and the Church of England Temperance Society.

In 1898 a temperance demonstration at Kit Hill Castle attracted "more than 2,500 people ... including a large contingent of children belonging to the Band of Hope and representatives of the temperance societies in Callington and the surrounding district".[CT]

Blue Ribbon Movement

From 1880 to 1882 the cause of abstinence was revived by the Gospel Temperance or Blue Ribbon movement, which originated in America. Amazing figures were claimed for renewal, new and juveniles pledges. In south-east Cornwall the main drive was in the first part of 1883 when a campaign was

Poster produced by James Venning of Callington, 1912
CHC Reference: 1997.041.009

inaugurated. At the end of January at a meeting in Liskeard, 126 took new pledges, 458 old abstainers renewed their pledge and there were 377 junior pledges.[CT] Two weeks later at Quethiock, "30 persons put on the blue ribbon".[CT] At the same time in Callington "455 new pledges were taken and 130 teetotallers put on the blue ribbon". In April in Callington another meeting urged "all to wear the Blue Ribbon and showed how in a large number of instances it had been the means of doing a vast amount of good. They considered it the duty of all to do all they possibly could to put down the traffic in intoxicating drink".[CT]

The temperance movement in all its many formats continued as an active part of society in south-east Cornwall up to the First World War. Entertainments, meetings, parades and outings were an integral part of the moral and social activities of the period.

At the beginning of the First World War the temperance movement received an unexpected boost due to state intervention when the Defense of the Realm Act was passed in 1914. According to the provisions of this act pub hours were limited, beer was watered down and was subject to a penny a pint extra tax.

Between the wars American exponents of their National Prohibition toured the country, to be met with derision and even violence. In the end the complete failure of Prohibition in America put paid to any remote chance that the temperance lobby would succeed in achieving its aims in the UK.

Temperance Achievements

Just what did the temperance movement achieve in Cornwall over a period of almost one hundred years and how did it affect the drinking patterns of the populace?

Membership

Membership of temperance societies and the number of converted drunkards are very difficult to calculate. In 1883 Mr. Bennetts wrote in the 'Methodist Temperance Magazine', that "Cornwall was the scene of some of the grandest triumphs of the early temperance advocates; as early as 1838 there were 18,000 teetotallers in the county".[24] Being a keen supporter of the movement these figures may well be optimistic, but with Cornwall having a population of over 340,000 in 1841 they would represent just over five percent of the population. Brian Harrison in his book on 'Drink and the Victorians' examines numerous figures and comes to the conclusion that by the 1860s there were fewer than one million teetotallers in England when the population for England and Wales stood at twenty and a half million. However he mentions that "the membership of many of these societies comprised mainly the converted; sober tradesfolk, church and chapel people, who were already temperate in most sense of the term .... Even at the peak of the campaign for personal reclamation in the 1840s, and relying on temperance sources, which if anything, exaggerate the movement's achievements – the largest proportion of reformed drunkards to ordinary members seems to have been no more than one in ten[25] .... Far from initiating a national reformation, teetotalism from the 1840s gradually became a way of drawing a line between the righteous and unrighteous".[26]

Reform

One of the chief criticisms against the temperance movement was that it had become a 'respectable' church organisation, doing little to reform the life of the drunkard and the circumstances that contributed to the problem. By the 1870s many temperance associations had paid lecturers and a small fee was charged to hear such speakers. In November 1868 a 'Cornish Times' correspondent displayed a degree of insensitivity to the poor with his comment about a speaker who was 'employed' by the Temperance League and gave an address that was "remarkably plain and the line of thought pursued by the lecturers interesting to the less intelligent portion of the audience".

Although the movement itself concentrated more on converting than reforming, there were many individual teetotallers who were active in reform movements. Temperance was soon adopted by working class movements fighting for the right to vote, who hoped abstinence would lend them an air of respectability. Throughout the Victorian era there was temperance participation in anti-slavery, anti-Corn Law, education, savings banks, prostitution, housing, working conditions and sanitation reforms. It was all these factors coming together that helped to improve the conditions of the working poor.

Legislation

An area in which the temperance movement was unsuccessful was in the political arena with their attempts to change legislation. From 1853 when the prohibitionist group the United Kingdom Alliance was formed, this hard-line group of prohibitionists was opposed by other temperance organisations that preferred moral persuasion to a legal ban. This division in the ranks limited the effectiveness of the temperance movement as a whole. In 1859 a prototype prohibition bill was overwhelmingly defeated in the House of Commons.

Sunday Closing

This was an important issue in Cornwall from the 1850s onwards. According to Bennetts, "Cornwall had the honour of being the first English county to demand by the voice of an enormous majority of its electors, the closing of public-houses on the Lord's-day". In 1854 the Cornish were celebrating some initial success when the Sale of Beer Act which restricted Sunday opening hours was passed, but within a short time it had to be repealed, following widespread rioting. Lobbying on this issue continued for several decades. In 1868 the Central Association for Stopping the Sale of Intoxicating Liquor on Sundays was formed. In 1882 there was a united move throughout Cornwall to achieve Sunday closing. At a meeting in Callington in February there "were about 600 were present, a resolution was enthusiastically passed without a single dissident in favour of Sunday Closing for Cornwall".[CT] However the combined force of the breweries and licensees' protective associations submitted counter petitions and the bill was blocked at its second reading in October of that year.

For over forty years from the Beer Act of 1830 to the 1872 Act there was little achieved in the way of legislation to assist the temperance movement. The 1872 Act, [see Chapter 1] was, to most teetotallers, a failure as it achieved so little in the way of restrictions to the alcohol industry.

Pub Closures

Although the national temperance organisations never came out with a policy encouraging local branches to close public houses by objecting to licence applications, it is clear that in Cornwall this did happen, by the actions of individual and organisations.

In Callington the application to re-license the *Wellington Inn* in 1875 was partly defeated by "a petition". There was a co-ordinated campaign against the *Forester's Arms* by the United Temperance Societies in Callington, between 1881 and 1883, when first a petition with 200 signatures was put forward, and then in 1883 when they finally succeeded, a petition with 500 signatures was presented. They are also said to have closed the *Royal Oak* which was in the same road [Church Street/Lower Street]. The *Ring O Bells* was closed in 1867. William Dingle, a prominent Methodist in the town, inherited it from his mother in 1849 and it was probably the influence of his wife Arrabella which caused him to close it and later to give it to the Methodists as a Manse. In March 1895[CT] when Mrs. Delbridge died there was a concerted effort to close the *Coachmaker's Arms* as "the house was not needed" and "was simply a tippling house". In this instance they did not succeed.

Efforts to close pubs continued into the twentieth century with the 'Cornish Times' reporting in March 1903 that there were moves in nearly every parish to reduce or completely close all public houses. In nearly all cases petitions, or 'memorials' praying that the Bench did not renew the licences, were handed in. In Callington these were presented by the rector, the United Methodist Free Church and Wesleyan ministers. The campaign continued in 1904, when the Chairman of the Magistrates refused to listen to the memorial presented by the Rector, the Bible Christian Minister and others. These efforts continued up to the outbreak of war when it was suggested that the licence of the *Market House* "might be done away with".

Temperance sympathisers were also responsible for the closure of inns in the parishes around Callington.

Attitude to drink

One of the greatest achievements of the temperance movement, which is seldom documented as it cannot be quantified, is the effect their movement had on people's attitude to the drinking of alcohol. Before the temperance movement, alcohol was an integral part of everyone's life and drunkenness was common both among the working classes as well as the middle and upper classes. The movement helped to show, by example, that alcohol was not essential to life, either as a stimulant to hard labour or even as a medicine.

Along with the religious doctrines, especially Methodism, excessive drinking was expounded as a sin. It took many decades, and was of course assisted by the changing Victorian moral attitudes and the ready availability of cheap non-alcoholic beverages, for drunkenness to become socially unacceptable. However one could debate whether this was ever achieved as once again drunkenness in the form of 'binge drinking' is a cause for concern.

Superscript abbreviations
CT   Cornish Times
SM   Sherborne and Yeovil Mercury
GAZ   Royal Cornwall Gazette
WB   West Briton
DR   Street or Postal Directory

1. George Sims, *How the Poor Live*, Chatto & Windus, Picadilly, 1889
2. H L Douch, *Old Cornish Inns and Their Place in the Social History of Cornwall*, D Bradford Barton Ltd., 1966, p.106
3. A K Hamilton Jenkin, *Mines and Miners of Cornwall Vol, XII*, Truro, 1966, p.184
4. Brian Harrison, *Drink and the Victorians*, Faber & Faber, 1971, p.184
5. T Hudson, *Temperance Pioneers of the West*, National Temperance Publication Depot, 1888. Accessed at the Cornish Studies Library
6. *Cornwall Teetotal Journal*, believed to be 1839, p.37, Cornish Studies Library
7. All references in this paragraph are St. Dominick Select Vestry Minutes, 30th May 1856 & 23rd March 1857, Cornwall Record Office, DDP/50/8/1
8. Harrison, p.179
9. P T Winskill and F R Lee, *The Temperance Movements and its Works*, Blackie, 1891
10. Douch, p.108
11. P T Winskill and F R Lee, p78
12. All references in this paragraph from *Callington Doctors*, published by Callington Heritage Centre, 2009
13. Harrison, p.300
14. George Bishop, *Bottles and Flagons*, 1995, published by Callington Heritage Centre
15. *The History of Tea in Britain*, www.britainexpress. com/ History/tea-in-britain.htm
16. John Wesley, *A Letter to a Friend Concerning Tea*, London 1748. Available to read on the internet
17. Harrison, p.39
18. Harrison, p.184
19. Charles Booth, *Life and Labour of the People of London*, 1902
20. Mary French, *A Victorian Village*, Falmouth, 1977, p.85
21. St. Dominick Temperance Rooms Membership Book 1898-1899, CRO, DDP/50/2/58
22. Natalie Allen, *A Stitch in Time*, N. R. Allen, Saltash, 1984 p.47
23. W R Stephens Account Book 1914-1928, in the ownership of Alastair Tinto
24. P T Winskill and F R Lee
25. Harrison, p.316
26. Harrison, p.194

CHAPTER 4

Callington, the Town with Too Many Pubs

By Lynda Mudle-Small

Callington, like many rural Cornish towns owes its existence to agriculture and the market. The charter for a market was granted in 1267 and until the 1960s when it closed, it was a very important feature of life in the town. Sheep and the wool trade were important industries during mediaeval times up to the Victorian period and the weekly sheep market was held where the police station now stands. Without it, and the regular trade it brought to the town, from a wide area, Callington, with its shops, trades and inns, would not have developed as it did.

Callington's position, at the junction of the road from Plymouth to Launceston and the north coast and from the east through Tavistock to Liskeard and the west was critical and played an important part in its development and the growth of its inns and public houses. The distance to most of these towns was within the requirements of stage coaches who needed a fresh team of horses every ten miles or so.

The other major influence on the town came in the early nineteenth century when the mining boom reached Callington. Only one mile north at Redmoor, Kelly Bray and Holmbush was a large mining area, part of which had been worked from the seventeenth century.[1] To the west was the large mining area of Caradon, then there was an area stretching through Kelly Bray, over Kit Hill and Hingston to the Tamar which was one huge mineral working area. At one time mines sprung up everywhere. In Callington there was an influx of miners to work these deposits, with two thirds of them coming from further west.[CS] The mines and the miners had a huge influence on the development of the town.

The Market Town

As our title indicates, Callington has had a lot of inns, especially in relation to its population. The market was one of the main reasons for this as it would draw people in from all the adjoining parishes, giving additional trade to inns and shops. It was the only livestock market between Tavistock and Liskeard and Launceston and Saltash, therefore farmers and butchers would come from a wide area to buy and sell stock and to discover and talk about the latest news. In addition to the weekly market there were four fairs a year, and a cattle-market every month, as well as an agricultural meeting once a year.[2]

When the lease of the *Bull's Head* was advertised in February 1748[SM] a selling attraction was that Callington "hath an exceedingly fine weekly Market on Wednesdays, and three great Fairs yearly". Ten years later when the lease for the *Red Lion* was advertised in June 1758 "a very large Stable" was mentioned as being "of great Advantage to a Tenant on Market Days". [SM]

The 'large stable' was necessary as visitors to the town would need hostelries with stabling. The yeoman farmer could tie his horse and trap to some posts near the market field but, at a time when horse stealing was not unknown, he would much prefer to leave them at the local hostelry stables and possibly adjourn there for refreshment before travelling back to his own farm. The requirement for stabling is mentioned in licence applications in newspapers.

In October 1838 [WB] when John Wenmouth applied for an inn licence he said that there was a house adjoining which might be made into a stable as he had "heard people complain of want of accommodation in stabling". In September 1872[CT] when a licence was applied for the *Railway Inn* at Kelly Bray due to the opening of the new railway, it was stated that "20 or 30 carriages or wagons went to Kelly Bray daily, and there were no places for the horses to be stabled". The licence was not granted that year as there was only accommodation for six horses at that time and "stabling and everything else wanted should have been erected before the licence was asked for". In September 1883[CT] when the *Forester's Arms* in Lower Street was struggling to retain its licence the defense pleaded that, "it had been a licensed house for a great number of horses, which was needed, especially on market-day".

The Transport Centre

Prior to 1750 the roads in Cornwall were so bad that the only travellers were those with essential business, this included the postal service. The first official post to Callington appears to have been authorized in 1722 when the Okehampton-Looe cross post service was established "the agent or sub-deputy at Callington [probably an innkeeper] received a salary of £5 per year".[3] For many years the main routes into Cornwall were the north route that went through Launceston, Camelford, Wadebridge and St.

Columb down to Truro and the southern route which went from Okehampton, Tavistock to the Tamar, through Callington, to Liskeard, St. Austell and Truro.[4] This placed Callington in a strategic position to its advantage. The central route over the moors was regarded with apprehension even though in 1754 a Bodmin innkeeper, had at his own expense "erected milestones for twenty-two miles over the large moors, which lay between Launceston and Bodmin".[SM] In February 1749 the *Bull's Head* was advertised as being in "a town situate on the Borders of Devonshire, and a great Thorough-Fare into and from the said County of Cornwall".[SM]

In 1764 the First Turnpike Act allowed for repairing and widening several roads leading from Callington. Three years later in May 1767 a mail service was inaugurated from the *New Inn*, Exeter every Tuesday. Thursday and Saturday for the *King's Arms* and *Standard Inn*, Falmouth, along the southern route which went through Callington. This would have been a great event to Callington, even though the post coach would have stayed no longer than for a change of horses at the *New Inn*. The mail coach would complete the Exeter journey in a day and a half at a cost of £1 10s. In March 1769 John Thorne & Co. set their coaches to travel from the *Bear Inn* in Exeter to the *New Inn* in Truro in two days; the fare from Exeter to Callington was 12s 6d., with the total journey being £1 5s 0d.[5]

The cost of travelling by mail coach was about 1d. a mile more expensive than by private stage coach, but the coach was faster and, in general, less crowded and cleaner. Toll gates had to be opened at the sound of the post horn for fear of a fine, so that the mail could go straight through. Mail coaches did not stop for refreshments, just for the change of horses and the exchange of mail bags. They changed their teams approximately every ten miles but this depended on the facilities and the terrain. For example, Tavistock was almost fifteen miles from Callington and with some steep valleys, but the *Royal Oak* was a staging inn on the Devon side of Newbridge which would provide fresh horses for the long climb up to St. Ann's Chapel, making these two stages about seven miles each. The average speed for a route would be around 7-8 mph in summer, dropping to 5 mph in winter. Travel on the mail coach was nearly always at night; as the roads were less busy the coach could make better speed.[6] It requires a little imagination to visualise the mail coach galloping into Callington with the sweating horses having completed the stage from the Tamar with the long uphill climb to St. Ann's Chapel. The horn would sound to warn everyone to keep out of the way and the coach would probably enter New Road and then drive into the cobbled yard behind the *New Inn*, to leave shortly after, as soon as the horses were changed and the mail bags

delivered, by the front arch into Fore Street and away to Liskeard.

The private stage coaches, such as those operated by John Thorne, competed with the mail coach. Crowding was a common problem with private stage coaches, which led to them overturning; the limits on numbers of passengers and luggage prevented this occurring on the mail coaches. Although referring to a mail coach this quotation from Dickens gives some idea of the difficulties of eighteenth century travel. "He walked uphill in the mire by the side of the mail, as the rest of the passengers did, not because they had the least relish for walking exercise, under the circumstances, but because the hill, and the harness, and the mud, and the mail, were all so heavy, that the horses had three times already come to a stop".[7]

Unfortunately for Callington, in 1787 the mail coach started to use the Bodmin moor route, but by then Callington was firmly established as a part of the southern route. Callington was situated at an appropriate 'stage' from Tavistock and the Tamar and Liskeard, and therefore the town's coaching inns [also referred to as coaching house or staging inns] were well situated to be a vital part of the inland transport infrastructure. The coaching inns stabled teams of horses for stage and mail coaches and replaced tired teams with fresh teams. When journeys were so uncomfortable, it was not surprising that travellers on the stage coaches welcomed all the stops for the change of horses, and the opportunity to rest their weary limbs and obtain some refreshment at the chosen inn under the patronage of the coach company. There was fierce competition for this profitable custom and the ability to provide good clean accommodation and ample stabling was important.

The *New Inn, Red Lion, Bull's Head* and the *Three Cranes*, all in Fore Street, had stabling provision and were all well placed to take advantage of this traffic, although we do not know that the *Three Cranes* did. The *Wellington* was also in Fore Street and had stabling provision, so was probably one of these staging inns, although it may have had another name in the eighteenth century.

There was further business for most inns in the provision of their own post-chaises which were available for general hire. These could be used by clients who were travelling privately in stages to their destination or for local excursions. In October 1768[SM] Richard Hambly of the *Bull's Head* is advertising that he keeps a post-chaise and in March 1778 William Porter of the same inn was advertising "that he keeps a Genteel Post-chaise and Good Horses". When widow Ann Porter gave up the *New Inn* in July 1786[SM] she made a point of mentioning that the post-chaise had only been run for a few months. One of her successors at the inn, Joseph Whitley in April 1797[SM] advertised "Neat Post-Chaises, Saddle Horses &c. &c". A bill from the *New Inn* dated May 1836 includes the sum of 9s paid by Sir George Stroud's agent, for the hire of a gig to travel from Callington to visit the Stroud properties in South Hill parish. In 1846 the service obviously continued, when the *New Inn* had become *Golding's Hotel*, as the 'West Briton' reported an accident:- "On Saturday night last, a post-chaise belonging to Mr. Thomas Golding, of the Hotel, Callington, was upset near Lumborn. The driver was thrown to the ground with such violence he did not live above ten minutes after the accident. An inquest was held the next day; verdict, accidental death".

Accommodation was also a requirement for anyone doing a journey of more than a day. In February 1749 when Samuel Winter left the *Bull's Head*, amongst the furniture for sale were "very good beds [most of them new],"[SM] and in April 1771 William Porter was advertising "genteel accommodation".[SM] In 1797 Joseph Whitley at the *New Inn* was announcing the "provision of new beds and every means to make the house comfortable". The *New Inn* had an advantage with accommodation as they had eleven lodging-rooms available.

In the nineteenth century there was a continuing expansion of carrier services with the omnibus being used from the middle of the century. These travelled a predetermined route from inn to inn, carrying passengers and parcels. This removed the need to book in advance, as had been the practice with stagecoaches. The omnibus featured wooden benches that ran down the sides of the vehicle; passengers entered from the rear. The various directories of the century give details of all 'carriers' and the routes they took and the frequency of journeys. Nearly all started and ended their journey at an inn.

Although the advent of the railway, which arrived in Cornwall via Saltash and then Liskeard to Truro in 1852 heralded the end of the mail coach, it would not have affected Callington too much, as there was still plenty of scope for carriers to connect with the train journeys, allowing travel to all parts of the country at a speed and in a degree of comfort that was unbelievable at the time. *Golding's Hotel* still advertised themselves as a 'posting hotel' in 1883, so maybe they had the contract for collecting the mail from the railway, or perhaps the term had just come to refer to post-chaises. The horse drawn services continued until the advent of the motorized vehicle. In Callington it was the Bond family who were owners of *Bond's Commercial Hotel* who became the first to offer a motorized omnibus service.

The Mining Boom

Miners have been a part of the Cornish landscape for centuries and there are traces of mediaeval tin streaming on the sides of Kit Hill.[8] However the mining boom came with the introduction of steam machinery that allowed the pumping out of water and the mining of greater depths. The expansion in the population of Callington and adjoining parishes came in the 1840s and rose dramatically until the 1870s. The effect the mining population had on the existing residents has already been mentioned in Chapter 3 and is also discussed in Chapter 5 and 6. In Callington it caused an increase in the size of the town with housing being at a premium, leading to considerable overcrowding. Shops and trades increased to meet the need and of course, premises selling alcohol also multiplied.

The Old Inns

In this instance I have defined an 'old' inn as one that was in existence before 1800. From mediaeval times all towns and parishes had an abundance of ale-houses and inns. In 1649 the justices instructed that the eleven or more inns and ale-houses in Stokeclimsland, be reduced to two.[9] - Callington is likely to have had an equal, if not higher number due to its market.

Right up until the mid nineteenth century Callington could be described as a small town bounded by three roads or lanes i.e. Fore Street, Church or Lower Street and Back Lane. In the seventeenth century its population has to be an estimate; in 1641 ninety one men signed the Protestation Oath, this number can be roughly multiplied by four to allow for women and children, this gives us 360 to 400 people, which by the first census in 1801 had doubled to 819. Therefore, in the 1700s when the population was something between 650 to 800 people it is surprising to find a mention of at least eleven inns, of which we can be fairly certain that five or six of them were in business for most of that century. This gives a ratio of around one to one hundred and if you take the children out of the equation the ratio is even lower. Jennings[10] estimated a ratio of one licensed premises to 90 people in 1700 rising to 1:207 by 1800, so Callington was on the high side.

Throughout the eighteenth century, as in previous centuries, the market would have drawn extra custom for the inns, but it was not until the middle of the century that transport routes improved. However the local inns would be used for various meetings; the court leet would meet in them and vestry meetings were in the habit of adjourning to the local hostelry.[11]

The *Red Lion, Bull's Head, Three Cranes & New Inn*, all had the capacity to be coaching or staging inns, and all predated the arrival of the first mail to arrive in Callington in 1722.

Bull's Head

In Callington the *Bull's Head* vies for the title of being the oldest inn, some saying it is as old as the church [1438]. However finding written evidence of this is very difficult. It may well have been a church house constructed in the fifteenth century, its proximity to the church gives this theory some creditability, but to date there is no actual evidence. There are stories of tunnels between the church and the inn, but what would be the purpose of going to all the effort of constructing a tunnel when there was nothing illicit or illegal about church ales? English Heritage, when they listed the building in 1968, considered it to be "circa early eighteenth century, possibly with earlier core. Remodelled circa late eighteenth century and extended to rear". The Callington Heritage Centre has a copy of a 1722 map of the town, made in 1930 by a local historian.[12] it shows the inn marked as "Morris Tenement called *Bull's Head*", it covers a large area in relation to adjoining properties and a 'gateway' is shown on the church side. The first landlord we have any knowledge of is Samuel Winter who in 1748 retired, at this time the inn was described as "an ancient house". Of course what the eighteenth century idea of an ancient house is, is open to question, but at least a hundred years is a reasonable guess, taking the *Bull's Head* back to around 1650. Samuel Winter made his will in the October of 1748 and died the following March leaving land in Crediton to his widow, one son and two spinster daughters.[13] Edward Keast took over and stayed for a seven year term, [the option of seven, fourteen or twenty-one years having been advertised] until 1761 when he moved to the *White Hart* in Callington. He was followed by William Porter who had been a servant of Sir John St. Aubyn, he announced his arrival in the 'Sherborne Mercury' in April 1771, soliciting the privilege of serving "such nobility, gentry &c. as shall please to honour him with their commands". In 1778 he was advertising post-chaises and then in 1783 he moved to the *New Inn* and Henry Rundle took over for a ten year term. In March 1790 Henry announced an enlargement of the premises.[SM]

As the century turned, the next landlord we know about is Henry Bullen who was in possession when the lease was advertised for sale in 1808 for a period of 99 years on the death of three lives. On the reverse of the sale poster the bids were noted, with some well-known Callington area names bidding; Mr. Werring, James Jope, Agrippa Wadge, Mr. Hornabrook, Jeff. Dingle, Miss Davy, Wm. Moon, N. Martyn, Sargent. Bids started at £50 and finished at £205 a long way short of the reserve of £450[14]. [What happened with the lease we cannot be certain, but in 1872 it was in the names of Edward, Thomas and Nick Bowhay, who were local brewers in Albaston]. Our next reference comes from the St. Mary's Church vestry minutes[15] when a mention is made in 1821 of the meeting adjourning to "the *Bull's Head Inn* kept by James Crabb." From the apprentices register, we see that James Crabb is assigned Mary Ann Rapson [12yrs] in 1818 and Elizabeth James [14yrs] in 1830 as apprentices.[16] We know that Philip Davis was landlord in 1840[DR] and 1841[CS] and may have been there earlier. Thomas Carpenter was landlord in 1844[DR] and in 1847 was commended for the "excellent dinner" provided to the Callington Cricket Club in September 1847[WB]. However he also had time to pursue his other trade as in the 1851 census he is described

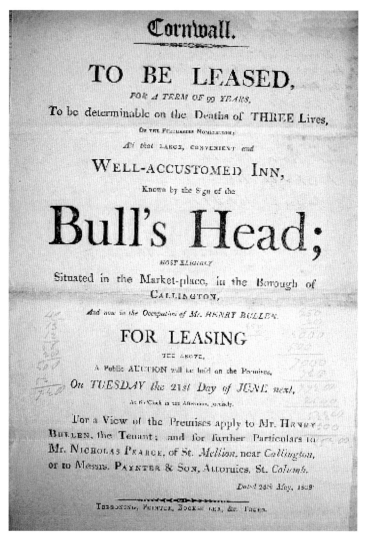

1808 Poster for sale of leasehold of the Bull's Head. Reproduced courtesy of the Cornwall Record Office. CRO CY6453

as an innkeeper and mine agent. The following four landlords all stayed for very short periods, John Jackman, David Cock, Charles Williams and Henry Bullen. In the 1850s the local carriers were busy and used the *Bull's Head* as a pick-up point, for journeys to Camelford, Plymouth and Saltash. John Brown moved from the *Coachmaker's Arms* to the *Bull's Head* after 1857 and continued to 1871 when he died at the age of only forty-one years. His widow Jane continued for another couple of years. The next landlord to stay a reasonable period was George Lakeman between at least 1885 and 1893, William Rundle or Rundell stayed until 1906. After a couple of short term licensees' Mr. William Dustan arrived in 1914 at the start of one World War and left in 1939 at the start of the second war. He is the first landlord of which there is a photograph and he saw the change from the provision of stabling to the garaging of motor vehicles. On the 8th May 1952 the licence was transferred to Sidney Ghey, who along with his wife Vera had come from Southampton. Sadly Sidney died in 1959 but Vera remains the landlady until this day. At 102 years she may well be the oldest landlady in the country and the fact she has been the licensee of the same inn for almost sixty years is probably another record. The *Bull's Head* will hopefully continue for a few more centuries yet, but the record she has achieved will remain as part of its long and intricate history.

Red Lion – Bond's Commercial Hotel – The Old Clink – The Phoenix

The *Red Lion* is also a very old inn. The building is shown on the 1722 map, at the location there is one building without anything written on it and the second with "R Treise Tenement". However in June 1758 [SM] when John Laws was the tenant, The *Red Lion* is described as a "very ancient and well accustomed house". The same problem exists as referred to with the *Bull's Head* being "an ancient inn". Just what was considered ancient in Georgian times? Assuming that 'ancient' is at least one hundred years, it does seem likely that the *Red Lion* may go back to the 1650s or even further. It had a strategic position at the west end of the Fore Street, next to the turnpike gate which is clearly shown on the 1793 map of the town.[17] At this time the courtyard is shown and although the land belongs to Lady Orford the tenant is still a Treise, this time Charles. The only other information we have for the eighteenth century is the Henry Vivian mentioned as landlord in March 1777[SM] who is possibly the husband of Elizabeth Vyvyan, a victualler, mentioned in the British Universal Directory of 1791.

From the 1830s to the 1860s the *Red Lion*, under various landlords does not seem to enjoy a good reputation in the local newspapers. In 1838 Wm.

Bond's Omnibus outside the Hotel in Callington in the early 1900s
CHC Ref: 1995.077.033

Henwood, the landlord, watched some drunks beat a policeman senseless in front of him. In 1842 Thomas Lake, landlord, was acquitted of an assault. In 1846 he was the victim of a theft by someone staying at this inn. In 1848 the new landlord, Sampson Jasper, who had moved from the *Royal Oak*, was again the victim of theft of porter and other articles. The next two landlords, Robert Sanders and John Hawkey were family men, both putting announcements in the paper when their wives gave birth. In 1858 there was another theft and in 1859 when Arscott Maker was probably landlord there was a theft case involving a lady of dubious morality who had 'picked up' a miner in the inn. In 1864 Arscott was fined for "permitting drunkenness and disorderly conduct in his house".[CT]

In 1868 the image of the inn changed when the Bond family arrived and it was renamed as '*Bond's Commercial Hotel*', probably by its name suggesting that it was a more economical alternative to the *Golding's Hotel* and suitable for the expanding number of commercial travellers. The inn enjoyed a period of stability under William and then Percival. They also ran a carrier business, William describing himself in 1881[DR] as a 'Mail Contractor and Coach Proprietor'. They were one of the very first to have a motorized vehicle in Callington which they used for their carrier service. When the Bonds left between 1926 and 1930 the property was owned or leased by C W Blundell & Co., brewers of Plymouth and in 1852 passed to the Tamar Brewery and then to the Courage Brewery, in 1963. During all this period there was a regular change of landlords. On the 1st April 1965 the name was changed from the *Commercial Hotel* to *The Old Clink*, after the Victorian 'clink' that was nearly opposite in the church grounds. Changes of landlord continued and at times the reputation of the inn was not good. In the last few years a new landlord changed the name to *The Phoenix* to indicate the complete change and renovation of the inn. Since then there have been other landlords and a landlady, and at the time of writing there is a for sale sign above the inn advertising the freehold for sale.

Three Cranes – Market House Inn
[now demolished and JS Tyres]

This is the inn that was built twice and demolished twice. We have no idea when it was first built, but it is clearly shown on the 1722 map as "James Hayes Tenement '*Three Cranes*'". It was situated adjoining the Guildhall or Town Hall which stood where the Spar shop is today. Despite the fact this was quite an old inn we have little reference to it. In 1793 it shown as belonging to Lady Orford and the tenant was David Horndon, but he is most unlikely to have been the licensee. In 1799 the lease was assigned to William Wearing.[18] In 1828 it was part of the Baring estate.

In the 1830's, *The Three Cranes* was demolished. It may have been very old and in need of complete rebuilding, or it may have something to do with the construction of the Pannier Market, which required an entrance on Fore Street. The adjacent Guildhall was demolished in 1832,[19] so it is likely the old inn was pulled down at the same time. The new building, was probably narrower than the original because of the Pannier Market entrance. An advertisement of the 6th January 1841[WB], tells us that the *Market Inn*, a free house, which is "an excellent and well-frequented inn" is "Newly-built" and that the present tenant, Mr. F Burnham "has been in possession of the premises for upwards of seven years". A "Convenient brewing-house", and stabling was attached. Mr. Burnham left in 1841 to go to the capital where he was innkeeper of the *Albion Tavern* in Bayswater Road in July 1844[WB] when his wife died. A postcard at the Callington Heritage Centre of circa 1890 shows the *Market Inn* as a small house, two storey [most Fore Street properties were three-storey], with three windows above and below a door to the left and a larger window to the right of it.[20] It would seem unlikely that this inn would offer accommodation, instead it would draw its income from stabling and the custom of local farmers on market days. It would have been named either after the new Pannier Market alongside it or the old market house that stood opposite, although this was also demolished about the same time. Shortly after Francis Burnham left in 1841, James Babb took over before moving onto another inn in Fore Street sometime around 1850. George Sargent and then his widow Emma held the licence until 1882, after which there was a regularly changing list of licensees. Apart from George Sargent, another two publicans died whilst working at the inn, this was a fairly frequent occurrence in the trade. In both instances the widow continued with the licence. From at least 1864 the inn belonged to Thomas Martin, a St. Dominic brewer and inn owner. In 1914 Mrs. Caroline Bowden [widow of Robert Bowden] was the last known licensee and in March 1915 the property was for sale, being bought by Mr. R Mortimore for £780. He turned the inn into a grocer's shop and later sold it to William Alford sometime in the mid 1920s, William had possession until after 1939. A photograph which must be late 1940s[21] shows it as Pomroys and also shows the front to have been remodelled with bay window above and the shop front added below. Eventually, once again, the building outlived its usefulness and was completely demolished around 1953, the area becoming first a garage and then a car tyre provider.

New Inn – Golding's Hotel – Blue Cap Hotel

In its time the *New Inn* must have been the most impressive structure dominating Fore Street, with it simple early Georgian style façade, decorated cornice and imposing portico, it extended the length

GOLDING'S HOTEL, CALLINGTON.

The imposing early Georgian façade of the New Inn which stretched from the portico on the left [which is still there], right across New Road to the chemists. The archway originally .gave access to the large cobbled yard and stables behind, although in this postcard, probably dated from the 1930s the stables had given way to motor car accommodation. CHC Ref. 1995.007.020

of eleven evenly spaced 16-paned sash windows on the first floor and at street level, along from the porch, was an arch leading to the extensive yard, brew houses and "fine eighteenth century stabling ...which could accommodate up to fifty beasts".[22] There was also an entrance off Saltash Road that led into the large cobbled yard. This was the start of New Road.

Again, our first reference to this inn is on the 1722 map where it is named as Nicholas Sargent's tenement, *New Inn*. Judging from the architecture the building may have been built within the previous ten years. In 1746 the Earl of Orford was rated for the inn[23] and a year later Jacob Geach's name appears as licensee. He kept the inn until his death in December 1763, when his widow May took over. By 1783 William Porter had moved from the *Bull's Head*, but shortly after, in 1785, he died and again the widow, Ann took over for a short period. By about 1790 Joseph Whitley had taken over and the story of his rise and fall has been told previously.[24] He had great ambitions for the improvement of the accommodation, post-chaises and even local roads, but by 1811 was declared bankrupt[25], with his family being looked after by the parish.

In June 1816[GAZ] William Golding, who had previously been a servant to Rev. Edward Clarke of St. Dominic, took over the *New Inn*. The Golding family, first William, then Thomas, Elizabeth and Frederick ran the inn, from Georgian times, throughout the entire Victorian era and on into the 1920s. By 1844 the *New Inn* had become known as *'Golding's family, posting and commercial hotel'*, a move that was common with many larger inns trying to establish themselves as not just drinking places but providers of "genteel" accommodation for travellers.

From a prominent location the family now ensured that the Hotel was central to numerous functions and activities in Callington. For many years their Assembly Room, which could accommodate over 200 persons, was the only large venue available in the town. Societies and groups regularly met at the Hotel, such as the Literary Institution, Agricultural Association, Rifle Volunteers, Cottage Garden Society, Turnpike Trust, etc. There were Auctions and surveys, inquests, tithe audits, talks, one-off meetings and entertainments all held there. Both Thomas and Frederick were also wine and spirit merchants as earthenware flagons still in the town testify. They were also farmers with Thomas in 1851 having 180 acres and twelve labourers. With over one hundred years of stability the Golding era can aptly be described as the golden period of the hotel.

In the 1930 Town Guide, A B Elford advertised *The Blue Cap Hotel*, "This Hotel for over 150 years was known as *Golding's Hotel*. It has now been completely modernized, All Public Rooms and Principal Bedrooms are Centrally Heated. Hot and Cold Water in Bedrooms. Cooking is done by Aga Stoves". He also promoted "an excellent garage and a Billiards room". Bed and Breakfast & Bath was 7/6d. Mr. Elford had been the Master of the Local Hunt in his native Cheshire and his favourite hound was named *Blue Cap* after the blue sheen on its head. Locals were not impressed that he did not choose a local name for the inn![26] In 1941 the *Blue Cap* was bought by the Plymouth Breweries and licensees changed every few years. In 1963 more than half the hotel, between the existing portico and the chemist shop, was demolished so that New Road could join Fore Street. The hotel struggled on for a few more years, before the property was sold and split up.

Today all that we have to remind us of this impressive Georgian hotel is the portico and what is now known as Golding's Flats. Rather belatedly it was listed as Grade II in 1986.

Wellington Inn

The *Wellington* is an inn which in September 1875 [GAZ] was described as "one of the oldest inns in the town", but there is little early information available. We know it had a prominent position in Fore Street being situated where the Post Office now is and in the building to the east of it. On the 1722 map it is not mentioned by name, and as the name of the

tenant of the time is not known, its early presence on the street cannot be confirmed. The first indication of the building is on the 1793 map where the position can be identified by the access to the rear at the side of it, but again it is not named. In the 1823 Pigot's Directory we have the first mention of the *Wellington* with Den Westlake as landlord. The 1828 map of the Baring Estate clearly shows the property with the access to the yard at the rear. From 1839 or before to about 1850 William Hodge was landlord and he was followed by Joseph Body. Joseph earned the patronage of several societies such as the Philanthropic Society and the Callington Tradesmen's Association and in November 1857[CT] he was personally involved in a pigeon shooting match with the landlord of the *Golden Lion* in Devonport. On that occasion between thirty and forty sat down to a "meal served up in Mr. Body's usual style". In 1861 Joseph Boddy [sic] is shown in the census as a retired innkeeper aged forty-six years, but in 1867 he shows up at the *Ring O Bells*. The 1861 census states Robert Sargeant was at the *Wellington Inn*. There was a sale at the inn in December 1863 so it was still operating as a public house then, but by 1869 an assignment of a lease[27] refers to "house, shop and offices in Fore Street, in the occupation of the Rev. F V Thornton, used as Reading Room and Institute". In September 1875[CT] an application for a new licence was made "for a house in Fore Street, Callington, known as the *Wellington Inn*. Some years ago this was used as an inn, but was afterwards let to the Rev. F V Thornton as a school house on condition that the licence was renewed yearly until an Act of Parliament prohibited the Bench from granting licences under such conditions". There were further details and the suggestion that Mr. Fairweather of the *Fountain Inn* would exchange that licence for the *Wellington*. The licence was refused. A petition against the licence was presented, believed to be from one of the temperance societies. By 1881 the property we believe had been the *Wellington* had been acquired by James Venning for his printing works. It was of course in a prime position in Fore Street and he was a prominent person in the temperance movement who was never slow to spot an opportunity! The front of the building has since undergone some changes.

One of the reasons for lack of earlier information on this inn may well be that the *Wellington* had a different name. The Duke of Wellington became popular around the time of the Battle of Waterloo in 1815 and many pubs were named after him. Some pubs changed names almost as often as they changed publicans and it may be possible at some date, when further evidence becomes available, to link the *Wellington* to an older inn in the town.

This sketch of 1881 shows the building that probably had been the Wellington Inn. In 1881 it was a printing works and was later changed to the current Post Office with a separate shop to the right hand side.

The Sun Inn, Callington. Photograph probably taken between 1906 and 1914. The gentleman with the dog is said to be William Solomon the proprietor. CHC Ref: 1995.073.028

Sun Inn

The *Sun Inn* is another old inn that instead of changing its name appears to have changed its location. It could of course have had an earlier name but in 1793 it is shown on the map as being on the south western corner of the main junction where the traffic lights now are. Margaret Congland was the tenant and she had been named as a victualler in the 1791 Universal British Directory as Margaret Congdon. On the 1841 tithe map the inn was on the north west corner and occupied a large part of that block between Back Lane and Well Lane.

The *Sun Inn* obviously benefitted from its position opposite the Sheepfair Meadow where the weekly market would be held. From the maps of the time it is difficult to make out whether there was stabling available and to date no advertisement for the inn has been found. It is likely there was stabling as from the 1850s it regularly features as a pick-up point for local carriers. There were a lot of short term landlords but some of those who stayed longer are; James Budge from at least 1823 to 1847 and John and then Elizabeth Paul from 1887 to 1893. John Matthew was the landlord from at least 1897 to after 1902. The Callington Heritage Centre has a photograph of William Solomon in front of the inn[28] early in the last century, he was the last known landlord, featuring in the 1914 Kelly's Directory, but missing from the 1919 one. Today the *Sun Inn* is the Pilgrim's Arcade of small shops.

Ring O Bells

The history of the *Ring O Bells* can be traced as its location in Church or Lower Street is known, it now bears the name Knoydart House and is adjacent to Lower House. The Dingle family were closely associated with the inn and the brewhouse adjacent and in 1762 when Jeffery Dingle married Sarah, he was described as "maltster of Callington". After Jeffery's death in 1825 in an accident, his widow continued to run the inn until she passed away in 1849, although William Crabb was shown as the licensee throughout most of this period. After Sarah's death Alexander Southey and John Gerrans were landlords until Joseph Body previously of the *Wellington Inn*, came out of retirement and took over prior to 1867. In September of that year he was fined for allowing drinking before 12.30 on a Sunday and it was stated that "No application was made for renewal of the licence of the *Ring O'Bells Inn*, Callington, as that house is about to be closed".[CT] Joseph Body died only a few years later in 1870 and was buried at Southill. His widow Susan went on to manage the *Forester's Arms*. When Sarah Dingle had died her son, William inherited and being a Methodist, he and especially his wife's temperance sympathies grew. The house was converted to a dwelling and later donated to the Methodist circuit as a Manse.

Bell Inn, Crown Inn, King's Arms, White Hart or Horse.

These are all mystery inns that date from the eighteenth century but for which there is only one reference or no known location. The **Bell Inn** is shown on the 1793 map. It was between the *Red Lion* and the *Three Cranes* and is simply described as 'J Sargents late *Bell Inn*'. To date, there is no other reference for it. The **Crown Inn** is mentioned once only in 1761 in some correspondence referred to in a file at the Courtney Library, where Benjamin Martin noted that John David, farmer's servant, of about twenty-two years was married to Mrs. Scott

A. Year	B. Licensed premises	C. Popula-tion	D. Persons per prem-ises	E. National average	F. Beer shops
1831	8	1388	173	168	
1841	8 + 3	1685	153	174	3 in 1838[WB]
1851	11 + 2	2142	165	188	Daw, Jago 1856[DR]
1861	12 + 2	2202	157	186	Bullen 1859 [CT], Peters 1863[CT]
1871	11	2173	187	201	
1881	8	1925	240	243	
1891	7	1888	270	276	

Data in column B compiled from census, directories and newspaper reports, includes beer shops and inns. Column C from census figures. E from Harrison 'Drink and the Victorians'. As beer shops do not feature in the census these details from newspapers and directories.

mistress of *Crown Inn* aged seventy-two. The **King's Arms** was in Lower Street and is mentioned twice, in 1798 and 1805, both times in connection with Joseph Whitley who was the landlord of the *New Inn* at that time. The 1805 reference regards a survey held at "the *King's Arms,* the house of Joseph Whitley," which seems to suggest that he was the licensee of two properties at the time. The **White Hart**, whose location is not known, is mentioned in July 1761 when Edward Keast placed an advertisement in the Sherborne Mercury to say that he had removed from the *Bull's Head* to the *White Hart*, "where will be good entertainment for Man and Horse, at the said House". In 1767 a survey was held at the house and it indicated that Theophilus Moon was the landlord. There is also a lease held at the Courtney Library dated 1761 that refers to the **White Horse**, is this the same inn or another mystery property?

It is quite possible that some of these earlier inns were simply renamed and continued in business. What was the earlier name of the *Wellington*? We know it was one of the oldest inns in the town, so before the Duke of Wellington there must have been another name. There is also the mysterious *Town Arms*.

Too Many Pubs? the 19th Century

During the nineteenth century the population of the town more than doubled from 819 in 1801 to 1714 in 1901 having reached a peak in 1861 of 2200. The first surge in the population came with the miners in the 1850s and 1860s, and then to meet the needs of the men and the mines shops, traders of all descriptions, and artisans expanded the population of the town. In 1851[CS] 42.7% of the inhabitants were not born in the town or the adjoining parishes. The mines started to decline from the 1860s and the 1880s and 1890s saw large numbers emigrating.

Apart from the existing old public houses mentioned above, new ones sprang up to meet the need. Then in 1830 came the Beer Act which allowed anyone with a ratable property, on payment of a two guinea fee to purchase a licence and set up a beer shop. A licence to sell spirits was five guineas. Beer shops sprung up everywhere, often without bothering with a licence. They are very difficult to trace as they were frequently transitory and were often part of someone's house. They do not feature in the Callington census, either because they were not legal, or they were run by the wife and it is only the man's occupation that is shown, or the man had two occupations; for example John Jago, who was a wheelwright is shown as also being a beer retailer in an 1856 directory, although only his wheelwright occupation is shown in the 1851 and 1861 census. A few beer shops have come to light through articles in newspapers and there are probably more to discover in the early newspapers. There are still memories of a beer shop, or kidleywink [the Cornish name for a beer shop] having existed in Laburnum Row up until the early 1900s. There is the same problem with inns. They could also be set up in houses and may only last a few years, thus never making an appearance in the decennial censuses. As we have seen names of inns can change and this makes tracing them difficult. Before new legislation in 1872, which required the house to be of a certain ratable value, inns could be established in any front rooms.

The chart above attempts to show the ratio of inns to population during the later nineteenth century. It is difficult to be accurate because of the reasons stated above, but the existence of illegal beer shops would have been national. This chart refers to licences for consumption on the premises and does not include wine and spirit merchants who were present in Callington. When you consider these figures refer to the whole population, of whom less than half would be adults you begin to come down to a ratio of less than one inn to one hundred people. The ratio for Callington is consistently below the national average.

This ratio, in comparison to modern times seems very high, it was even thought high by some of the population at the time as can be seen by the following newspaper article from the 'West Briton' of 26th October 1838, when John Wenmouth appealed against the decision of the magistrates not to grant him a licence for a public house in Callington, as he already had a beer shop he wished to upgrade to a public house.

"Stephen Pomeroy examined by Mr. Coode – Was bailiff at the Hundred of East, and attended the sessions at Callington on the licensing day, the 6th of September. [Two magistrates voted to give the licence, two voted against, and one did not give his reasons.] Witness was well acquainted with Callington. There were about 1,500 inhabitants, and eight public-houses. Wenmouth keeps a beer-shop at the north part of the town. It was capable of affording good accommodation; and there was a house adjoining which might be made into a stable. There was a large weekly market at Callington – four fairs in the year – a cattle-market every month, when there was no fair, and an agricultural meeting once a year. ... Witness believed another public-house would be a great accommodation, and had heard people complain of want of accommodation in stabling. By Mr. Lyne – There are three beer-shops, besides the eight public-houses in the part of the town where Wenmouth lived, there were three public-houses within a short distance. Mr. Lyne admitted the fitness of the applicant; but only questioned whether there was a necessity for a public-house. The Bench granted the licence.

So Wenmouth got his licence, and in 1842 we have proof from a newspaper article that he was landlord of the *Royal Oak*. This was in Lower or Church Street, but its exact location is unknown, it was possibly towards the Newport end as Wenmouth's beer shop is described as being in the "north part of town".

After this it was mentioned in the vestry minutes in 1844 when John Wenmouth was the landlord. Wenmouth seems to have left by 1847 and Sampson Jasper was there for a short time before removing to the *Red Lion*. Several other landlords feature with Mrs. Mary Peters, widow of William who was landlord for two years from 1858-1860, being shown in the 1861 census. Although in 1870 and 1874 Nicholas Proctor from Stokeclimsland and then Landulph is shown as the leaseholder on the Voter's Lists there is no evidence of the building surviving as a public-house into the 1870s. It does not appear in a list of licensees at the 1866 licensing sessions and probably closed before this. One theory that requires evidence is that the *Forester's Arms* may have taken over from the *Royal Oak*.

Newport Inn – Coachmaker's Arms

The *Coachmaker's Arms* is an existing Victorian inn. It was a purpose-built building erected by the Cotehele brewer, John Bickle, on land leased from Lord Ashburton in 1837. William Body is shown as a publican in the 1841 census. In June 1842[WB], the lease of the *Newport Inn*, as it was known at that time, was auctioned. At that time it consisted of the inn with a parlour, two kitchens, passage, bar and cellar on the ground floor and four bedrooms over a wash-house, stable, pig's houses and enclosed courtyard. Also with it was the newly erected brew-house and premises which were 34 feet by 20, [10m x 6m] stone built and roofed with Delabole slate. All the equipment was also for sale which included a copper brewing boiler that could hold 260 gallons [1185 litres], two working stillstands of

The Coachmaker's Inn circa 1910, painted in 1926 by Captain Symons

37 feet [11m] in length, vats, barrels, hogsheads, blocks and tackle and numerous other items of equipment. By 1846 William Jasper was the landlord. He was also associated with the coach-making business that operated in adjoining buildings and by 1850 the name of the inn had changed. The Jasper coach-making business grew apace, [it continued until 1900], and in 1856 the landlord was John Brown and in 1861 Robert Rendell took over. In 1870 George Delbridge was landlord and when he died at the age of thirty-five, his widow, Mary continued to at least 1893. There was a concerted effort to close the inn at this time by the parish council, District Councillors and "all the representative men in Callington,"[CT] but this failed. For the next thirty five years there were only three landlords; William G Bowden, George Humphrey and Mrs. Buckingham. After this landlords changed more regularly through the remainder of the twentieth century.

The Coachmaker's although on the main south/north route was very much in the tradesman's area of Callington. The 1906 ordnance survey map shows it surrounded by industrial buildings. Immediately to one side, on the south, was the Tannery and behind that the Gas Works. The coach-making buildings surround the other sides. At some point, possibly as early as 1852 when Thomas Martin of St. Dominic took over the inn, the brewery buildings were converted for use by the expanding coach business. There were two smiths nearby, a wheelwright works just up the road and a printing works opposite. Some of the coach-making sheds were used right up to the 1980s as agricultural equipment storage; they were the last commercial buildings to survive. Now the *Coachmaker's* is surrounded by housing.

Fountain Inn

The *Fountain Inn* was on Fore Street, not far from *Golding's Hotel*, alongside Biscombe Lane and currently used as Annie's Café. The earliest reference we have to it is in 1872 when it appears in the Register of Licences, with Robert Fairweather as licensee and the owners being the Misses Louisa and Mary Golding. In the 1871 census Robert is listed as a wine and spirit merchant. This would appear to be his main business which he also carried on from Saltash Road, but in September 1873 he did apply for his six day licence for the *Fountain Inn* to be replaced by a seven day one. In 1875 he was involved with the failed attempt to exchange his licence at the *Fountain* for the *Wellington*, [see above]. Shortly after this he must have left to concentrate on the wine and spirit trade. William Snell, another wine merchant was at the *Fountain* for a few years. From 1882 to 1893 John Spear appears as licensee. John was another wine and spirit merchant who also listed himself as a mineral water manufacturer. Between 1893 and

1914 there were three landlords listed under the *Fountain* in Kelly's Directories with no mention of being merchants. In March 1903 there was a failed effort to have the licence withdrawn, with the Anglican, United Methodist Free Church and Wesleyan ministers all handing in petitions. There were objections about the facilities, just a small tap room with no sanitary accommodation and no stabling. The owners, Plymouth Breweries promised to rectify the sanitary arrangements. After 1914 there is no mention of the Inn. It's earlier ownership by the Golding family is strange, as this allowed a competing wine and spirit merchant to have a Fore Street base right next to them.

Town Arms

Now this is one of the mystery inns, but we can make a guess as to where it was. In 1780 the 'Sherborne Mercury' mentions a survey at the house of John Toms, [unfortunately no inn name given]. John Toms is also listed as a victualler in the 1791 Universal British Directory and on the 1793 map of the town he is indicated in a building between the *Wellington Inn* and Well Street. The only time the name 'Town Arms' occurs is in the 1861 census, with James Babb as innkeeper, about eleven schedules [or households] along from the *Bull's Head*. We know James was at the *Market House*, probably until at least 1850 when the Ashburton Estate was sold. In an 1856 directory he is shown as a beer shop keeper and in December 1859 he "was charged with having his house open after 10 o'clock on the 4th November. P C Dymond visited the house about 11 o'clock, and found about thirty persons there drinking, this being the night on which an annual supper of the ringers of Callington is usually held in the house".[CT] His defense was that he could keep his house open until 11.00 which would be a public house licence but the magistrates decided it was only until 10.00 which were the beer shop hours. A later licensing session confirms he only had a beer shop licence even though he had the space to accommodate the Callington Ringers. Regardless of which licence he had, until more evidence comes to light the mystery remains. Was the *Town Arms* the same inn that John Toms occupied in 1780?

Forester's Arms

The *Forester's* or *Forrester's Arms* appears to be a short-lived public house in Lower Street. Mary Ann Peters was the wife of William who was the licensee of the *Royal Oak* for a short time, he died and in 1861 she is shown as the licensee, but by 1862 she had moved to the *Forester's*, as Mrs. Mary Ann Peters of the *Foresters Arms*, Callington, married Richard May at Stoke Damerel, Plymouth on the 29th September 1862. She obviously felt obliged to marry Richard as the birth of a son was announced on the 21st January 1863. The marriage appears to have been an unfortunate one as it was reported in

June [CT] of that year that "Richard May, of the Forester's Inn public house, Callington, was apprehended by Inspector Marshall, charged with beating and otherwise ill-treating his wife, Mary Ann May, and also with threatening to do her grievously bodily harm. On stating the case before the Magistrate the complainant said she wished to punish her husband for his brutal conduct, and also to bind him over to keep the peace towards her". Quite how she rid herself of her violent husband we cannot know, but by 1871 she was shown as a shopkeeper and a widow. Another widow, Susan Body, was at the *Forester's* in 1871. By 1881 Nathaniel Lobb was landlord but this was when the licensing difficulties referred to earlier occurred and the licence was lost in 1883.

The Railway Inn, Kelly Bray, circa 1900-1920

Kelly Bray & Newbridge

On the edges of the parish there were inns at Newbridge and Kelly Bray, although Kelly Bray belonged to Stokeclimsland parish until the 1930s. The inn at Newbridge was the building that faces west as you come down from St. Ive, crossing the River Lynher on the route up to Callington. In the early nineteenth century the main road swept round in front of the inn, rather than going straight up the hill as it does now. The inn is not shown on the 1841 tithe map, but in 1847 the *Newbridge Inn* is shown on a list of ratepayers. Throughout its existence it belonged to David Horndon of Pencrebar, the large house between Newbridge and Callington. The two main publicans were Robert Keast in the sixties and seventies and George Gregory until 1889 when the Register of Licences records that the Licence was not applied for at the 1889 Annual Licensing Meeting.

Apart from Kelly Bray Farm, Kelly Bray is not an old settlement. The 1841 tithe map only shows a few cottages down in the valley in Winsor Lane that were probably associated with the mining. The original Kelly Bray inn was the *Winsor Arms* at the west end of the lane. Throughout the 1850s to when the licence was not renewed in 1879 the landlords were William Peters, James Peters and Mrs. Peters. In May 1872 a railway line was opened from Calstock to Kelly Bray, this was for transportation of ores and goods, the passenger facility not coming until the next century. It made a huge difference to Kelly Bray and warehouses,

shops and dwellings soon followed. In 1872 Silas James saw an opportunity and applied for a licence for the property that stood on the junction of the Stoke and Launceston roads. He failed to get this in 1872 as he did not have adequate stabling provision, but in the following year the *Railway Inn* was opened. In the 1880s and 1890s the licence was held by John Dingle, who owned the sawmills over the road. In the 1920s to the 1950s Samuel and then May Skews were landlords and locally it is remembered that "Sammy Skewes, was a popular figure with the locals when they popped in for a drink". In the 1960s when the railway line was closed the inn name was changed to 'The Swingletree'. Being a brewery house there has been a regular turnover of licensees in the latter part of the twentieth century.

The Mystery Inns and Innkeepers

With the rapid turnover of inns and publicans and changes of names, it is inevitable that over one hundred and fifty years later not all of them can be traced. Some may be due to journalists and directory errors, especially where we only have just the one reference.

The **Crosskey** is mentioned just once, in a newspaper article in 1863 which referred to a fraud case. The **Hare & Hounds** in Lower Street is mentioned twice in 1847 in a directory and a list of ratepayers. **Wright's Hotel** appears just the once in an 1845 newspaper article when it apparently hosted a meeting of the East Cornwall Agricultural Association. Joseph Andrews appears as an innkeeper in the Apprentices Register in 1805. Henry Hutchins innkeeper of Lower Street and Edward Timewell innkeeper of Fore Street appear in the 1841 and 1851 census but we have no inns or beer shops for these three.

As we have seen, the temperance movement was responsible for the closing of public houses in Callington such as the *Foresters, Royal Oak* and *Wellington*, and indirectly the *Ring O Bells*, but they were not the only cause of the town that had too many pubs in 1838, having almost half the number by the end of the century. From the peak in 1861 the population of Callington was declining, many miners and their families emigrated and with the expansion of trades and shops, and the success of the Methodist movement the town became more 'respectable' and probably needed less public houses. The houses that were closed were the smaller ones whose continued viability may have been questionable.

The Twentieth and Twenty First Centuries

The first few decades of the twentieth century saw more casualties as the *Market House, Fountain Inn* and *Sun Inn* closed their doors for good. A hotel was no longer viable and although *Goldings* struggled on as the *Blue Cap,* it eventually succumbed to the requirements of the motoring population for better roads. However what has expanded are the 'teetotal' options, as it is now possible to be served a non-alcoholic drink in at least five different venues in the town. 'Refreshment rooms', in the form of restaurants and take-away establishments have also expanded. Callington now has over three times the number of people it had in the middle of the nineteenth century and just three public houses, the *Bull's Head*, the *Phoenix* and the *Coachmaker's*. May they continue to prosper for a few more centuries.

Superscript abbreviations
- CT   Cornish Times
- SM   Sherborne and Yeovil Mercury
- GAZ   Royal Cornwall Gazette
- WB   West Briton
- DR   Street or Postal Directory

1. A K Hamilton Jenkins, *Mines and Miners of Cornwall Vol, XV,* Truro, 1965, p.36
2. West Briton 26th October 1838 in reference to John Wenmout's appeal against licence refusal
3. David B Cornelius, *Devon & Cornwall, A Postal Survey,* The Postal History Society, Reigate, 1973, p.24
4. H L Douch, *Old Cornish Inns,* Bradford Barton, Truro, 1966, p.66
5. References in this paragraph from the *Exeter Flying Post* accessed by Douch in his book above
6. *Mail Coach Services,* Postal information leaflet published by the Heritage Trust, 2005
7. Charles Dickens, *A Tale of Two Cities,* Chapter 2.
8. *The Archaeology of Kit Hill, Survey Project Final Report,* 1988, Cornwall Archaeological Unit, p.15
9. Assize 24/20 Order Books, Public Record Office
10. Paul Jennings, *The Local: A History of the English Pub,* The History Press, 2011
11. Callington Churchwarden's Accounts 1750-1819 CHC Ref. 1995.008.005, also at Cornwall Record Office [CRO]
12. Plan of Callington 1722, copied by William Paynter in 1933 from unknown source, CHC Ref. 1995.019.028
13. Will of Samuel Winter, Public Record Office B/11/769
14. Bull's Head Inn sale poster, CRO CY6453
15. Callington Churchwarden's Accounts 1750-1819 CHC Ref. 1995.008.005
16. Callington Apprentices Register 1802-1835 CHC Ref. 1995.001.001, also at CRO
17. A Plan of the Borough of Callington 1793, CRO N436
18. Assignment of Lease from Jn. Sargeant to Wearing, CRO Y/1857
19. J Venning, *Vennings Directory Map & Historical Notices of East Cornwall,* Callington, 1935
20. Postcard of Fore Street CHC Ref. 2006.600.243
21. Photograph of Fore Street, CHC Ref. 1996.078.019
22. From English Heritage Listed Building details No.
23. 1746 Rating details, Devon Record Office 72/17/12
24. *Callington Heritage Centre Newsletter* December 1990
25. *Taunton Courier,* 11th July 1811
26. Recollections of John Tonkin, CHC Ref. 2010.119.004
27. Assignment of lease 1869, Devon Record Office DD CY 94
28. Photograph of Sun Inn, CHC Ref. 1995.073.028

CHAPTER 5

Parishes Without Pubs

By Miranda Lawrance-Owen

There were so many alehouses in the parish of Stoke Climsland in 1649 that the local justices were instructed to reduce them from over ten to just one or two[1] and in the small parish of South Hill there were at least three pubs during the eighteenth century. Today the parishes of South Hill and Stoke Climsland are the only ones in the Callington area without a single surviving pub. This chapter briefly examines the rise and fall of the pubs in the two parishes and tries to explain why they appeared and why they are no longer there.

The two parishes were probably much the same as any other community in the church centred drinking times of the mediaeval period. There is some evidence from seventeenth century glebe terriers[2] to suggest that both parishes may originally have had mediaeval church houses: the South Hill terrier records that apart from the Parsonage house, two barns and a stable, there was "a small house also on the north east of the [Parsonage] house with a hall and a cellar, a chamber over the hall, and a chamber over part of the cellar". The description sounds very much like some of the Church houses in existence today. At Stoke Climsland the terrier is even more explicit. At the north-west corner of the churchyard, there was "another dwellinghouse containing a hall and a shop, a buttery, a small slee house at the east end, the hall only with a chimney, two chambers above with a chimney, planched, a newly erected stable and pigs house and a little orchard and a herb garden, all usually set at annual rent by the rector as a Public Inn". No documents have been found to indicate when the 'public inn' in the corner of the churchyard at Stoke Climsland ceased to function, but by the mid eighteenth century there was a *'New Inn'* in the village. This building was across the road from the church and later became the *Half Moon* pub. One of the earliest innkeepers was probably Robert Harvey at whose 'house in Stoke Climsland Churchtown' a 'survey' was held in 1722[3] We do not know whether Harvey's 'house' was the old one in the churchyard or the *New Inn*, but by 1763, the Clarke family were running the *New Inn* and remained there until the early 1800s when first William Hawton and then the Grigg family took over. Members of the Grigg family ran the inn for over forty years.

By the time of the 1841 census, there were at least six drinking establishments in Stoke Climsland parish, four in the main village area, one at Bray Shop and one in Luckett. There may well have been others whose proprietors carried on other trades as well and did not include both occupations in the census. This would have been particularly likely after the Beer Act of 1830 made it easy to set up small beer shops.

Catherine Grigg, a widow aged fifty, was 'innkeeper' of the *New Inn* where she lived with her son Thomas aged twenty, three daughters and two female servants. Thomas took over the inn a few years later and appears in a strange case in the local magistrates' court following the theft of a duck from his inn, which was later found dead in the skittle alley. The thief, a labourer by the name of Richard Maddeford, was sentenced to hard labour for one month.[4] Simon Philp, aged thirty, a brewer living in Stoke Climsland Village in 1841 appears next but one to Catherine Grigg's household in the census

Stoke Village today. The building on the left was the Half Moon Inn with the door to the inn being just to the left of the drainpipe. Where the Social Club stands on the right there used to be a three storey stone house

return but we cannot be sure where his property was. Also in Stoke Climsland village was William Perkin [or Parkin], aged fifty and listed as a 'brewer labourer'. John Doidge, 'publican' had been running the *King's Arms* at Bray Shop with his wife Mary for at least three years and stayed there for another thirty years, and Samuel Floyd, 'innkeeper' with his wife Thomasin and three small children was at the *Maltster's Arms* in Luckett, purpose-built as an inn in the early 1830s. Finally there is a tantalising reference to a 'Cider House' somewhere in the parish, run by one John Eggsford who was also the victim of a theft, in January 1841[GAZ].

By 1851, there is no trace of the *Cider House*, but the other five innkeepers or brewers were still there plus James Skinner, a sixty-five year old 'maltster' and his lodger William Lord listed as a 'maltster and brewer'. Five years later, in 1856, Kelly's directory lists four new drinking establishments in the parish, the *Winsor Arms* at Winsor run by the Peters family for the whole of its twenty three year existence and three 'beer retailers': a Mrs. Clarke of Stoke Climsland village and H. Bonman and R. Sowden both in the hamlet of Tutwell. It also lists an S. Clenic as proprietor of the *Half Moon Inn*, ending the long tenure of the Grigg family.

It is difficult to be sure exactly how many drinking establishments there were at any one time because the censuses only provide a snapshot and several places may have come and gone in the intervening years. Similarly, although the various trade directories can fill in some of the gaps, they are still only snapshots, not always reliable, and of course the very small or perhaps less reputable houses might never appear. However, by cross checking the censuses and trade directories, together with other sources such as newspaper reports, we can be reasonably sure that by 1856 the parish of Stoke

Climsland once again had at least eleven drinking establishments of various sorts, a similar number to that considered to be so objectionable by the government in 1649.

1856 appears to mark the high water mark for the pubs of Stoke Climsland and numbers began to decline after that. The 1861 census records only seven individuals running licensed premises: William Francis was now at the *Half Moon Inn* with his wife and daughter, all of whom came originally from the Truro area. In 1861 Francis was charged with using defective measures and a few years later they moved on to Linkinhorne where they ran a pub there. Simon Philp appears as a 'farmer of thirty acres', but a newspaper report of the sudden death of his wife Elizabeth in 1864 gives his occupation as 'brewer and maltster', so we can assume he was still trading but with a second occupation which was the only one he chose to record in the census. John Doidge and William Peters remained innkeepers of the *King's Arms*, Bray Shop and the *Winsor Inn* respectively and the *Maltster's Arms* was still in Luckett, now run by John Gumb, a thirty nine year old 'Innkeeper and Blacksmith'. There is no mention anywhere in the census of James Skinner, William Parkin or the three beer retailers listed in Kelly's Directory five years previously, but a Mrs. E Clarke appears in the census as a carpenter's widow, so she may have been the beerseller and may well have continued her trade despite not listing it in the census. However, there are two new individuals in the list – James Rowe, aged forty-six, appears at a new establishment, the *'Ring O' Bells'* in Stoke Village with his wife and twenty two year old son. James is listed as a 'Grocer and Brewer' and his son George is listed as a 'Brewer', so the family appear to have combined the two businesses as a family enterprise. It is possible that Simon Philp previously ran the *Ring O' Bells*, but this is unlikely since he seems still to have been trading as a 'brewer and maltster' in 1864, by which time James Rowe was certainly at the *Ring O'Bells*. Ten years previously James Rowe was listed as a 'Grocer Tailor', so he was obviously a man of varied skills. He and his wife and son seem to have continued running the *Ring O'Bells* until his licence was refused in 1873 after he had been fined for 'keeping late hours'. The second new licensee in the 1861 census was William Rowse, a 'Tailor and Beer House Keeper' aged twenty eight. His premises are not named in the census and it is difficult to know where his beer shop would have been, but wherever it was it was probably crowded as he shared it with his wife, two children, his brother and sister in law and their

A view of Luckett Village with the minehouse in the background. The Maltster's Arms is the building above the heads of the group of children who are in the foreground. CHC Ref. 1996.003.010

three children. Rowse is listed only as a tailor in the following census ten years later, but we do not know whether his beer shop closed down or whether he was yet another licensee with two occupations, only one of which was recorded in the later census.

When the 1871 census took place, only five official licensed premises remained in the parish, the *Half Moon*, run by copper miner Simon Sleep and his wife Ann, who subsequently carried on the business alone for six years, after his death in 1872; The *Ring O'Bells* which appears to have closed by 1873; the *King's Arms* still run by the then widowed John Doidge until about 1873 when Walter Martin took over for a few years until it too seems to have closed; the *Winsor Inn* and the *Maltster's Arms*. John Gumb was still at the *Maltsters* in 1871, but soon after that Kelly's Directory of 1873 lists the landlord as William Peake. Peake had married the original innkeeper's widow, Thomasin Floyd, and after her death in 1876 her eldest son John bought out his brothers' and sister's shares in the pub[5] and he took over and ran it until 1888.

The census returns and Kelly's directory confirm that only the *Half Moon* and the *Maltster's Arms* survived after 1881. The Floyd family appear to have sold the *Maltster's* to the local Bowhay brewery in about 1888[7] and John Tucker took over as licensee, combining running the pub with strawberry growing. By 1901 one Henry Woolridge was licensee and according to contemporary newspaper reports he ran "a very poor house" and was the subject of numerous complaints. When a Mr. Bennetts took over from him in 1904 he had great difficulty persuading the magistrates to renew the licence because of the bad reputation the pub had gained during Woolridge's tenure. Bennetts was successful then, but eventually the *Maltster's Arms* fell victim to the campaign to close 'unnecessary' pubs. The magistrates refused to renew its licence, apparently because the population of Luckett was not large enough to justify its continuance[6] and it closed in 1913. The *Half Moon* did not survive long into the twentieth century either, its eventual demise being brought about by the Temperance movement. It was bought by the Tavistock Brewery at some time during the tenure of Harry Bassett who was 'Innkeeper' by 1881. Bassett and the Inn survived the sale of the Tavistock brewery including the *Half Moon* in 1899 and Bassett remained there for twenty years until some time after 1902 when Luke Boundy took over. However, when the pub next came on the market it was apparently bought up by a group of local Methodist families with the sole intention of allowing the licence to lapse, and it too closed . Time had finally been called at the *Half Moon*. By the time of the Second World War it was being used as a hostel for Land Army girls and eventually became a private house. The story goes that once the *Half Moon* closed, anyone in Stoke Climsland wanting a drink had to walk to Horsebridge or Kelly Bray "and they did too".[8]

The much smaller parish of South Hill, less than half the size of Stoke Climsland in area and about one third its size in population, does not seem to have had any ancient inns. This may have been due in part to it being an area of scattered farmsteads and hamlets with no large village community until the growth of Golberdon in the nineteenth century. There could have been some individual brewers who have faded from the record, but with the possible exception of the reference in the seventeenth century Glebe Terrier to a mediaeval Church house, the earliest record so far found of an inn in South Hill is an advertisement dated 4th July 1834 announcing that a tithe meeting would be held at the *New Inn*, Golberdon. We do not know how long the *New Inn* had been in existence by the date of that meeting, but we do know where it was. An advertisement for a meeting in 1840 records that the *New Inn* was run by Joseph Rogers. According to the tithe map[9] Joseph Rogers lived in a property in The Square, Golberdon, which still exists as a domestic house. The freehold owner of the property was William Golding, owner of Callington's *New Inn* for many years. Surprisingly, the inn was next door to the Bethel Methodist Chapel in Golberdon, which was originally situated in The Square[9] before the building of the present [now converted] chapel in about 1864. The Bethel chapel was in existence by about 1818,[10] so was possibly there before the *New Inn*. If so the *New Inn's* arrival must have caused considerable controversy.

The 1841 Census does not mention the inn and only lists Joseph Rogers as a 'Smith', aged forty, living with his wife Anne. Once again, it appears that innkeeping was a dual occupation and the inn may have been run by Rogers' wife. Rogers was still at the *New Inn* in 1851 when the census records his occupation as 'innkeeper and blacksmith', but after that the inn was taken over by John Rich, who had previously been innkeeper of the *Royal Oak* in Callington. Rich remained at the *New Inn* for over

Owners and Occupiers Of Land

IN THE

Manor of Callyland

GENTLEMEN,

IN consequence of the last crop being nearly taken off Golberdon Common, and the contract entered into by the Tenantry of the Manor no longer binding on the parties, we (the Committee) who were appointed to manage relative to the Tillage thereon, think it necessary to appoint a Meeting of the Owners and Occupiers of Land in this Manor to devise a plan for the future stocking of the said Common. We therefore request that all Persons interested in the concern will meet at the *NEW INN*, Golberdon, on FRIDAY, the 18th of JULY instant, at 10 o'Clock in the forenoon, for that purpose. We also further request that all Persons who have not paid their proportions for keeping the said Common safe from trespass will pay the same to Mr. Moorshead, on or before the day of Meeting, when the Account will be produced and settled.

| Signed | J. H. Trehane | Wm. Wenmoth | Wm. Dunstan |
| | John Smith | John Hendy | John Hicly |

Dated July 4th, 1834

J. VEALE, Printer, Bookseller, &c. CALLINGTON.

A poster from July 1834 giving notice of a meeting at the New Inn, Golberdon.

twenty years until it was taken over by his wife, after his death in about 1877. The two censuses during his tenure reveal that he was another dual occupation innkeeper with trading as a carpenter as his other source of income. There are various newspaper reports and advertisements about auctions and meetings held at the *New Inn* during Rich's tenure, which suggest that it was a typical centre for community activities. The South Hill Friendly Society in June 1862, held their annual dinners there for example; about one hundred people sat down to dinner at the inn after a church service for which they used to "marched in procession" from the *New Inn* to the Church at South Hill and back, "preceded by the South Hill Band".CT In May 1863 the newspaper report was fulsome in its praise for Rich. The marchers apparently "enjoyed a substantial dinner got up in a manner highly creditable to mine host of the *New Inn*". The diners included the Rectors of South Hill and Stoke Climsland and various local magistrates.CT

By 1863, however, Rich had competition in Golberdon, in the shape of *The Farmers Inn*, run by Thomas Rowell, who appeared as a 'publican' for the first time in the 1861 census. Thomas Rowell had previously been a 'Farmer of 44 acres' and he and his wife and children lived with his parents elsewhere in South Hill parish before moving to the *Farmers Inn*. The name of the establishment suggests either that Rowell the former farmer set up the *Farmers Inn*, or he may have carried on farming while running it – perhaps he saw it as an opportunity to move his family to their own place after sharing with his parents for so long, but he did have his widowed father in law living with him by 1861. The *Farmers Arms* was probably not as 'respectable' as the *New Inn* – in February 1863 Rowell was convicted of

'keeping late hours' and fined £5 and costs, apparently not his first offenceWB and from this report and subsequent censuses and directories it seems that the *Farmer's Inn* was a beer shop, rather than an inn.

It is difficult to be sure exactly where the *Farmer's Inn* was in Golberdon, but by correlating census schedules with the tithe map and apportionments it seems likely that it was one of a number of buildings, now demolished, which once stood in the middle of what is now the main road through Golberdon towards Pensilva, either on the edge of the square or nearer the cottages on the other side of the road, opposite to the *New Inn*. Thomas Rowell remained at the *Farmer's Arms* until his death in 1875, when it was taken over by Richard Pethick, previously a 'Blacksmith and Navy Pensioner' living in Golberdon. Four years later, in September 1879, Pethick moved to take over the *New Inn* – an example of a beer shop keeper moving up in the hierarchy – and as "no-one came forward" to take over the licence of the *Farmers Arms*, the renewal of its licence was formally refused and the *Farmers Arms* closed.CT

The only other licensed premises recorded in South Hill parish was the *Rising Sun*, a beer shop established in Maders some time after the passing of the Beer Act in 1830 but before May 1857, when it was advertised for sale as a "Dwelling House [consisting of eight rooms] now occupied by Mrs. Stone, widow, on a licence for the sale of beer".CT The premises had originally been the gatehouse or toll house at the edge of the road across Golberdon Common, owned by Lord Ashburton, but subsequently bought by the Bowhay brewery. The 1857 advert noted that the house was "peculiarly adapted for the sale of beer, situate in the centre of Callington Mines, among a mining population and on a traffic thoroughfare".

It sounds as if the *Rising Sun* might have been aimed at exactly the type of customer so feared by many in Cornwall, such as the Gazette writer of January 1835 who commented on "the riotous conduct of the profligate frequenters of those pests of the Mining Districts, the beershops" The purchaser of the premises was John Worth, a miner born in Tintagel who had probably moved with his miner father to Stoke Climsland where he married a Stoke Climsland girl.[11] Worth and his wife managed to keep the beer house going until 1877 "despite frequent complaints against the house", but in October the magistrates finally refused to

The New Inn occupied a central position in the village of Golberdon, it is now a private dwelling

The dwelling in Maders that was once the Rising Sun and features in the advertisement on the right

Advertisement from the Cornish Times 3rd May, 1857 for the sale of the Rising Sun, Maders.

renew Worth's licence after a conviction for "selling liquor during prohibited hours on a Sunday"[WB] for which he was fined £1 [considerably less than the fine Thomas Rowell received in 1863]. Despite the complaints, the police had apparently found it "difficult to detect anything wrong" at the premises because of its "situation at the end of a common" – probably a classic case of the difficulties in securing convictions in respect of such premises, referred to earlier in this book.

Following the closure of the *Farmers Arms* and the *Rising Sun*, the *New Inn* in Golberdon was the only pub left in South Hill parish. In about 1883, after Richard Pethick's death, it was sold to the Vaughan Brewery of Saltash, later Plymouth Breweries, and was run for almost ten years by a Mrs. Jane Chamberlain, wife of George Chamberlain, a 'Naval Pensioner' like Richard Pethick. Robert Taylor then took over for a few years until his death in 1897, when he was followed by John Ball, previously a farmer from Trenavin near Golberdon, who rather grandly styled himself 'Hotel Keeper' in the 1901 census. The *New Inn* finally closed in 1903, a rather surprising victim of the campaign to close pubs deemed to be 'unnecessary', following the Farnham Magistrates case of 1902. In March 1903 a total of nine public houses in the Callington Licensing Division were objected to for various reasons, only two of which related to the condition of the premises and none appeared to relate to misconduct of the houses. The main objections seemed to come from members of the various churches in the area, many of whom had signed petitions for the closure of their local pubs. Well known local Methodist lay preacher and solicitor, Isaac Foot, represented the objectors in almost all of the cases, in five of which strong representations were made by local church leaders. Opposition did not come, as might have been expected, only from the Methodists. In the case of the *New Inn* at Golberdon, the Rev. Shaw, Rector of South Hill with Callington, gave evidence that he

"thought the house unnecessary. He had a petition signed by 190 inhabitants over eighteen years of age against the renewal, a very large majority of the parishioners being in favour of the house being closed". When questioned by Mr. Pearce, solicitor for the licensee, why he wanted to get rid of the only public house in the parish, he said that the parish wanted to get rid of it and admitted, to laughter from the court, that he wanted to get rid of it too and that he thought "it would be desirable to abolish public-houses". Mr. Davey, chairman of the Parish Council, said "the house was not required in the village, where there were twenty three householders, of whom sixteen were teetotallers". Another parishioner, Mr. Rogers, "considered that a great deal of harm must be done to the people who visited the house" and Mr. Coad said "the feeling in the parish was overwhelmingly strong against the renewal of the licence. He had nine years experience as a Guardian, and had seen sufficient to convince him that public-houses were injurious to public morals and produced pauperism". The licensee's solicitor bravely fought on, requesting the renewal of the licence because the *New Inn* "was the only public-house in the parish. It had existed for over sixty years, and the witness[es] had not brought forward a single stain against it" but the religious objectors won the day and "the unanimous decision of the Bench was that the *New Inn*, Golberdon, was not required, and the licence would not be renewed". None of the other eight pubs suffered the same fate, despite similar objections and despite the fact that none of the others was the sole pub in a parish or village. The claim that the pub was not needed because most of the residents of Golberdon were teetotallers, seems a little unfair to the residents of other parts of South Hill parish, because the total population of South Hill parish at the time was around five hundred people, only one hundred and ninety of whom had signed the Rector's petition. What the other two hundred or so adults thought about their only pub closing, we do not know, but no doubt they, like the residents of Stoke Climsland, would have walked to pubs in their neighbouring parishes, in this case Linkinhorne, Callington and St. Ive.

The parishes of Stoke Climsland and South Hill are similar in being rural, largely farming communities, each with numerous scattered hamlets and farms. However, the larger area and population of Stoke Climsland – over two and a half times the area of South Hill and around three times its population at any one time – seems to have enabled it to produce and sustain a surprising number of pubs, some of them for many years. Mining was blamed for the "multiplicity" of alehouses in Stoke Climsland in 1649,[12] but it was not until the early nineteenth century, following the opening of the various mines in East Cornwall and on the Devon/Cornwall border that the mining boom really hit the Callington area. It is generally assumed that it was the influx of miners which produced the rapid growth in pubs and beer shops in Cornwall. Was this also true for Stoke Climsland and South Hill? In Stoke Climsland parish it is clear that at least eight of the licensed premises which appear in the records almost certainly opened during the mining boom – the *Maltster's Arms*, Simon Philp [both 1830s]; the *Winsor Arms* [1850s]; James Skinner [1840s/early 1850s] and the beer shops of Mrs. Clarke, H Bonman and R Sowden [all 1840s/early 1850s] and William Rowse [1861]. Two others probably opened at that time: the *Ring O' Bells* [in the 1850s] and the *King's Arms* at Bray Shop, first recorded in 1838, although it may have opened earlier. Only the *Half Moon* was definitely in existence before the Victorian mining boom.

In South Hill parish all three of the licensed premises seem to have opened between 1830 and 1860. The *Farmers Arms* and the *Rising Sun* definitely opened then and the *New Inn* probably did so, as no record of it has been found before the 1830s.

These dates correlate strongly to the increase in the mining population in both parishes. The highest census population in both parishes between 1841 and 1891 occurred in 1851 – two thousand five hundred and ninety-six people in Stoke Climsland and seven hundred and thirty in South Hill. In the same year the population of people connected with mining [including wives and children] in both parishes went up to over three times the number in the previous census [to about three hundred and sixty-seven in Stoke Climsland and about fifty-one in South Hill]. In 1861 the population of both parishes fell slightly, but the number connected with mining increased by about eleven per cent in Stoke Climsland and more than doubled in South Hill.

By 1879, all the pubs in Stoke Climsland apart from the *Half Moon* and the *Maltster's Arms* had closed, as had two of the three in South Hill. This correlates

with a steep decline in the mining population. The overall population of both parishes was declining in all the census years after 1851, but not as fast as the decline in the mining population. Between 1861 and 1871 the mining population of Stoke Climsland went down by sixty two percent to one hundred and fifty two people and the general population went down by about five per cent. In South Hill, the mining population decreased by fifty nine percent to forty five people, whereas the general population went down by only seven percent. There was a slight increase in miners in Stoke Climsland in the 1881 census, but by 1891 the numbers were falling again. In South Hill the number of miners had almost halved by 1881 and although it went up slightly in 1891, by 1901 there were only seven people in the parish connected with mining. The 1901 figures for Stoke Climsland were not researched.

Overall, the conclusion for both parishes must be that there was a sudden increase in licensed premises between the 1840s and 1860s which was linked to the increase in people connected with mining. Once mining numbers declined, even though the overall population did not fall as fast, most of the pubs quickly closed, the inference being that it was the miners' custom which kept them going and the loss of that custom brought about their closure. Of the three pubs which survived the end of the mining boom, the closure of two was connected to the Temperance movement. The *New Inn* at Golberdon was certainly closed due to pressure from local Anglicans and Methodists and the *Half Moon Inn* at Stoke Climsland apparently closed as a result of Methodist action. It has so far not been possible to discover the details behind the decision that the *Maltster's Arms* was no longer needed, but it would be interesting to discover whether this too was a result of agitation by members of the local churches.

Superscript abbreviations
CT   *Cornish Times*
WB   *West Briton*

1. H L Douch, *Old Cornish Inns*, Bradford Barton, Truro, 1966, p.21
2. Glebe terriers are written accounts made by the minister and churchwardens of a parish about the parsonage house and all the land and buildings belonging to it. The Terriers for 1679/80 are remarkably detailed for both parishes.
3. Royal Institute of Cornwall, Notes of H L Douch, *Plymouth Weekly Journal* or *General Post*, 27th April 1722
4. Cornwall Record Office QS/1/44/728
5. CRO DD PP/677
6. Douch, p.204
7. Register of Licences CRO/JC/EMM1 D/26
8. George Bishop, *A Parish Album of Stoke Climsland*, 1987, p.24
9. Tithe map and apportionment for South Hill, 1840, at CRO
10. Ann Eade, From Bethel to Zion, Callington Museum, 1995
11. Stoke Climsland Marriage Registers, 14th June 1855
12. Douch, p.21

CHAPTER 6

A Taste for the Low and Vulgar

By Nikki Chaplin

"Amongst a mining population outrages frequently occur, and unhappily of a diabolical character. Drunkenness and vice abound to a fearful extent, and a taste for the low and vulgar in every sense is to be witnessed at all times and at all seasons. Visit a mining village or hamlet whenever we may, the eyes as well as the ears are pained with what invariably is to be seen and heard".[CT] Readers of this report into a fight in the village of Latchley in November 1860 were left in no doubt about the prevailing attitude of the day towards alcohol. The image is of a community disintegrating because of the demon drink. Working hard, and sometimes drinking hard, the mining villages began to get a reputation for rowdiness.

Although witnesses told the subsequent inquest that the protagonists, both miners, were sober, they had spent the evening of Saturday, 27th September in the *Rising Sun* in Latchley, where John Bodiner had been practising with the band, and it seems unlikely that they had drunk nothing. The argument erupted when Richard Piper made some comments about a couple of the local girls. "High words and angry altercations ensued and the two men accompanied by 200 persons adjourned to a neighbouring field where they practised pugilism with fierce and fast blows. During the fight Bodiner received a fatal blow and survived only a few moments. The man who dealt the blow was fearfully mangled, his face being a spectacle to behold and almost blind". William Stephens, a farmer of Latchley, stated that he was informed a fight was going on in his field but he did not think much of the fact because "fights were so common in the neighbourhood".[CT] The fight continued for an hour and forty minutes even though several people tried to stop it. Perhaps the most telling comment was that William Stephens ignored all reports about the fight as it was going on because it wasn't unusual. Needless to say the landlord of the *Rising Sun* lost his licence. William Stephens for his part was so exasperated by the rowdy behaviour of the miners that he persuaded the rector, Thomas Hullah, to hold Church of England services in his barn in Latchley and later he gave up a piece of land for the building of a Chapel of Ease, St. Michael and All Angels, completed in 1882.

Three years later, in August 1863,[CT] there was further disapprobation in the newspapers when Calstock's police constable Cole was beaten up by two drunken men, incited by others in the village.

His description of what had happened was reported in the papers "Almost immediately afterwards Warrick and Bennett came towards me in a fighting attitude. I had previously heard some conversation between the two men, and Bennett said to the other "Let us go back and kill the b*****," to which Warrick replied, "Yes, we will be the death of the b*****!" At the time they made use of the language I do not think they could see me. When they came towards me Warrick was in advance of Bennett. Warrick struck me right and left in the breast. Bennett followed him and struck me also. I drew my staff to defend myself. I saw Mr. Tregoning there and called upon his for assistance. He did so. I drew my staff after I had had several blows. They clenched me, and after a struggle I cleared myself of them. They rushed on me again, and others who were assisting me held them back. I put the staff in my pocket and took out the handcuffs. My assistants were knocked down, and Warrick then caught hold of me by the hair saying, "We will put the b*****s head in the barrel," which was full of water. They failed to do that, and they got me on the ground, and kicked me several times, from my head to my knees. I received a severe blow; which broke my nose. I saw Prout standing a short distance off, but I do not know that he did anything. The mob incited them to strike me. When I was on the ground Warrick and Bennett, and a third man whom I do not know, turned the barrel upon me, and threw water over me. I received a pair of black eyes, I was under medical treatment for some time". Two days later a mob gathered to try to prevent police constables taking Warrick and Bennett into custody, and they too ended up in court.

Although such extreme incidents were rare, there was deep concern about the level of drunkenness, and offenders, including the pub landlords themselves, often found themselves in court.

At Callington Petty Sessions in August 1859 "Robert Burley of Calstock, Richard Rundle and William Lea, were each fined 5s and costs, for being drunk and disorderly".[CT]

Newspapers reported the proceedings of the licensing committees, where magistrates frequently expressed concern about drunkenness, and also took consideration of the number of pubs needed in a particular locality before granting a licence.

At the Callington Brewster Sessions in September 1872 "James Bolt, keeper of the *Tavistock Inn*, Gunnislake, was objected to by Mr. Superintendent Barnes, who did not wish to close the house, as there are only four for 3,000 inhabitants, but who objected to the landlord. Evidence was given that the house was conducted in a disorderly manner, and that drunken men were seen coming out of it. Bolt was fined in November last for permitting drunkenness in his house, and three of the men that were there at the time were fined for being drunk and riotous. Several others had been convicted during the year for being drunk and riotous on the highway after leaving the house. Mr. E. Nicolls, solicitor, for the applicant, submitted that, according to the evidence of the police, the landlord had done his best to keep his house orderly, the constables having seen his removing drunk people. He had been convicted only once, although he had kept the house for a long time. The bench refused to renew the licence".CT

Eleven years later at the Callington Licensing Sessions in September 1883, there was an application for a new licence: "With reference to the alehouse licences Superintendent Barnes said he had something to ask about three of them. One was an hotel licence at Gunnislake, the licence of which he would ask might be allowed to stand over to the adjourned sessions. He felt it his duty to make this request in consequence of what had come to his notice. There had been an amazing amount of drunkenness in the neighbourhood. He was sorry to say that during the past year they had had fifty three convictions for drunkenness there, and they had eleven more cases that day, and a great deal of this he believed could be traced to the house in question - the *Tavistock Hotel*".CT

Later in the same licensing sessions, magistrates heard an application for a new licence for the *Ashburton Hotel* at Danescombe, the previous licence had lapsed when the holder left the area. Superintendent Barnes objected "not because he had any complaint against the house or intended tenant, but because a new house was not required. Two licensed houses were within a short distance of the incline or station, where the men were at work, so that the men would have to go only a short distance to get to houses already licensed if they wanted refreshment. A chief reason for objection was the excessive number of public-houses when compared to the inhabitants, who numbered 1,100 at the last census, and for whom there were six public houses, one for every 290 persons."

Magistrates also controlled opening times, and the population of the area was important in assessing how long an inn could stay open. Beer shops were only permitted in property above a certain valuation. In May 1875GAZ Thomas Cocking was fined for keeping his licensed premises open after hours, [past ten o'clock at night] and George Trevarton, Andrew Binley, John Millet, George Dodd and John Jewell were each fined 6d for being in the house during prohibited hours. Stephen Spettigue was fined in 1858 for falsely certifying that the house of Thomas Jewell in Latchley was eligible for a beer licence.

At the licensing session in September 1874, "The Chairman informed the innkeepers that Callington, Calstock Town and Gunnislake were the only three places in this division declared by the Licensing Committee to be populous places. The whole of the rest of the houses, therefore, would have to be closed at 10 pm".CT

Most contentious were the number of pubs in Calstock Town itself. Discussions in March 1903 about a licence for the *New Inn* centred around the size of the population and provide an interesting insight into the two sides of public opinion. "The police contention was, Mr. Foot pointed out, that the house was not required, the population of Calstock having decreased by 687 during the past 30 years. Inspector Roberts said there were six licensed premises at Calstock within a radius of a mile. By Mr. Peter: Three licences were quite enough for Calstock where there were about 2000 persons. He could not say that over 2000 people landed at Calstock in one day. Those who did had usually had plenty of drink before they arrived, as there were bars on the steamers. Rev. A Pidgeon, Baptist minister, who said he had been at Calstock seventeen years, said there were too many public-houses there. He would abolish them all. – Mr. Peter: You are a very unbiased witness. – [laughter] Mr. Peter said the house afforded considerable accommodation for persons who went to Calstock by boat. There was a good business done there, and it would not do to shut the smaller houses merely because a few teetotallers did not want them. He hoped that before long public opinion would right itself on the question of licensing. One was afraid that a great injustice would be done in consequence of this sudden desire to close a large number of public-houses: but it was evident that opinion was taking a more moderate line".

It is perhaps surprising that the miners had such a bad reputation for drunkenness when they made up the bulk of the congregations at the Methodist chapels. The Chapels extolled the virtues of temperance, and most had Bands of Hope. The ironically named Temperance George, born in 1796 in Metherhill, is almost a personification of the struggle between the drinkers and non-drinkers. She holds the essence of abstinence in her name; yet in 1861, after the death of her husband, she was listed as a beer house keeper at Netstakes between Gunnislake and Calstock. Her customers must have had some amusement being served beer by Temperance!

Before 1800

Beer and cider had been brewed and drunk in the parish of Calstock for centuries, for the most part viewed as a healthy alternative to water. The parish had an aletaster, who had the job of ensuring that beer measures were fair and that the ale was good. Beer is frequently mentioned in the oldest manorial court records for Calstock that still exist - from 1296 - when people were regularly fined for breaking the assize of brewing – probably for selling beer at below the statute price. In that year, Radulf Whyta and eight of his associates, together with Henry de Launceveton and eight of his associates were fined for false measure and breaking the assize of brewing[1]. The probate inventory for Calstock farmer, James Adam, dated 11 April 1602 mentions barley and hops which are likely to have been used for brewing.[2] But unfortunately the manorial records were only concerned with money they could raise from the parish, and do not go into any detail about the numbers or location of any alehouses or breweries. Ale was a staple drink for the mediaeval population as water sources were not always palatable. There is stronger evidence in Calstock parish, for the brewing of cider as an everyday drink, many inventories of Calstock folk include cider-making equipment, and this was mostly for home consumption. It is likely that ale was also brewed on some farms.

Soon after the Alehouse Act of 1552, there are entries in the manorial court records that indicate there were at least three inns in the parish at that time. In 1559 Richard Honeycombe of Harrowbarrow, Richard Hawke and Roger Want sought recognition for their inns – the license cost them one hundred shillings which must have been a fair amount at the time.[3] The exact location of these inns is impossible to establish, but it would be nice to think that one of these may have been the *Carpenter's Arms* in Metherell. It is hard to prove it was the earliest pub in the parish, but the building dates to the sixteenth century[4], and would have been one of the oldest stone buildings in the village. Claims have been made that workers employed to build the earliest buildings at Cotehele in the 1300s were put up at the *Carpenter's Arms*, and that is the explanation for its name[5], but no documentary evidence for this can currently be found, however it is a strong candidate as one of those early three inns. More likely is the explanation that the property later belonged to three generations sharing the name Samuel Hunn as they were all carpenters by trade.

The early inns across the parish are likely to have been the venue for public meetings; the manorial court met every three weeks, moving from village to village; pubs were still the venue for manorial meetings into the nineteenth century[6]. Public events like this and land sales and inquests were advertised in local newspapers once they started publication, and are helpful for providing information about the pubs from the 1700s.

Carpenter's Arms, Metherell
Photograph courtesy of Clarence Hunn

The *Carpenter's Arms*, for example, is likely to be the venue mentioned in the 'Sherborne Mercury' of September 1745 "at the house of Mrs. White in Metherhill" for a survey prior to the leasing of some land. The 'Plymouth Mercury' or 'General Post' of July 1722 mentioned "the house of Thomas Colling at Alson [Albaston]" when advertising the letting of the parish mills.

An inn that used to exist at Churchtown Calstock may also have been one of the earliest in the parish. There are references to an establishment "near the church" or "at Calstock Churchtown" throughout the 1700s. Looking at the buildings that still exist by the church nowadays, it is hard to imagine a small hamlet there, but there is a strong case for an inn to be part of any settlement. The Church was the gathering place for the old manor, and it would be likely that a central "social and administrative" venue would have been close at hand. In December 1796[SM] this was named more specifically as the *Duke of Cornwall's Arms* and from the 1760s to the 1780s the innkeeper was William Borlase[7]. In March 1793[SM] the innkeeper was William Alman. However, from the early 1800s other Calstock pubs were used for meetings; and William Almond, victualler, [probably the son of the William at Calstock], was at the sign of the *Cornish Arms* in Gunnislake from 1806 to 1821, so it seems likely that the *Duke of Cornwall's Arms* had closed by then.

An inn in the lower part of Albaston is mentioned in the eighteenth century, and may be the third of the early drinking establishments in the parish.

Inns linked to transport

It wasn't until the late eighteenth century that new inns linked to the transport routes are to be found. With Calstock Town becoming increasingly important as a port, it is not surprising to find inns adjacent to the river. Joseph Langman had been an innkeeper in Calstock when his death was announced in the 'Sherborne Mercury' of 21st June 1790. It is likely that he was the landlord of the *Waterman's Arms*, later the *Boatsman's Arms* and finally the *Tamar Inn*.

Inns were some of the first buildings to be put up alongside the Turnpike Road from Gunnislake New Bridge to Callington. The *Calstock Inn* [now the *Rifle Volunteer*] at St. Ann's Chapel and the *Cornish Inn* at Gunnislake [now the *Cornish Arms*] were both mentioned in the Act to improve the road in 1827[8], although neither building appears on the Gardner map of 1784/6, surveyed less than twenty years after the original Turnpike Act was passed,[9] however both are shown on the Davis map of 1815. It has been suggested that the *Tavistock Arms* in Gunnislake dates from 1704, but there is no structure shown at that location until the 1839 tithe map when it appears as a T-shaped building

The building projecting on the right in this busy street in Gunnislake advertises 'White's Temperance Hotel Baker, Confectioner and General Dealer'. Photograph courtesy of Calstock Archive Trust

occupied by three households. By the time of the first edition of 'Kelly's Directory' in 1856, it is certainly an inn, the *Tavistock Inn* run by landlord James Mudge.

Village expansion

The final major factor in the proliferation of licensed premises in Calstock parish was the huge expansion of various industries throughout the 1800s which brought rapid population growth. Gunnislake as an identifiable village didn't exist in the early 1800s. Inns and hotels, alongside non-conformist chapels, were put up as quickly as the houses in the mining villages. Some beer shops appear to have been built next to "hotels" which were more like hostels where miners newly moved to the area could lodge until they were settled. There were also small drinking establishments, beer shops – all seem to have had a checkered history with names changing and landlords falling foul of the licensing laws. In this period it was not just mining; quarrying, brickmaking and market gardening were all growth industries, particularly after the arrival of the railway line to nearby Plymouth in 1848. With men working long hours at hard physical jobs, it is not surprising to find pubs and inns opening up for their leisure time.

Coffee Shops and Temperance Hotels

The Bands of Hope and Rechabites were popular movements among the mining community in East Cornwall. As the movements grew in strength, Temperance Hotels and coffee shops started to appear in the villages alongside the pubs, inns and beer shops. Alfred Martyn was a grocer in Gunnislake, and he ran a Temperance Hotel [later coffee rooms] alongside his business from 1887 to 1906[DR]. He was also a Bible Christian minister. He was later joined by Frederick Williams who was a baker and also ran a Temperance Hotel in Gunnislake[DR]. A 1902 postcard of Gunnislake [page 54] shows White's Temperance Hotel on Commercial Street. Harrowbarrow, which seems to have favoured abstinence since there was no drinking establishment in the centre of such a large village, could boast a Temperance Society Coffee Tavern in 1881. At this time Calstock was a popular destination for river trips, and a number of refreshment rooms were opened. Harriet Richards started the trend with her refreshment rooms at Tamar View in 1889. Samuel Worth [also a bargeman] and David Penrose Webster are listed with refreshment rooms in 1893. The *Country House Inn* at Cold East [Coombe] above Harrowbarrow was the first pub to change itself into a Working Men's Club [1889].[DR] After the First World War, Gunnislake Working Men's Club appears in the directories, as does Chilsworthy Young Men's Club. In villages like Latchley, social drinking took

Mr. Stephens and the Harvest Festival fare upstairs at the Tamar Inn.
Photograph courtesy of Shirley Smale

55

place as well at informal gatherings in the cider poundhouse where the local men would get together, draw off some of the cider, and pass the glass around between them. As Gerald Pridham recalled, they would "call in a crowd tonight, and we'll see about some drinkin' and eatin". He reckoned "there was about a dozen went in there. There was three or four of 'em 'ad to be carried away".[10]

The pub and social gatherings

Just as the temperance movement became associated with the village bands that played in front of banner waving marchers promoting the pledge, at the *Tavistock Inn,* Gunnislake, so singing became associated in Calstock parish with the pubs. The men would walk to the pub on Saturday night at Gunnislake or St. Ann's Chapel ["up Turnpike"], and as they walked home to their villages they would sing on their way. In Gunnislake they would gather first in the village square: "Could be thirty, forty. All the men as they come out of the pubs they started singing, and was good singing. The Buffaloes [Ancient Order of Buffaloes] trained them see... Train 'em to sing over at the *Tavistock Hotel".[11]* As they walked through Gunnislake the local policeman, PC Elliott would be following quietly behind because singing in a built-up area would attract a fine. Ironically enough it was very often hymns that they sang and they harmonised into different parts as a matter of course. Maggie Dodd, who remembered this habit with fondness, used to

love to hear them as they stood at Windy Bridge near Chilsworthy before heading their separate ways: "They'd come to the bridge, twelve, half past, and sing – honest to God, it was beautiful – hymns, all sorts. I used to get out of bed to listen. Boys came home from Gunnislake one night, and he [Mac Pridham] was tight, and he would not move from Windy Bridge. They put Mac in the wheelbarrow, but he didn't want to go that way, he wanted to go the other way [via Cox Park]. Two of them had to hold him while the others wheeled the barrow".[12]

As well as providing venues for countless organisations to hold meetings, dinners and gatherings of every description, and for typical pub games such as darts, snooker, euchre and skittles, it became the practice in Calstock pubs during the early twentieth century to hold Harvest Festivals on the licensed premises. The *Queen's Head* Albaston, *Rifle Volunteer,* St. Ann's Chapel and *Tavistock Inn* in Gunnislake would receive boxes of enticing fruit and vegetables, all to be auctioned off amid an evening's socialising and drinking.

Calstock Pubs
Duke of Cornwall's Arms, Calstock Churchtown
[Exact location unknown]
Mentioned in eighteenth century newspapers, but likely to be older and possibly one of the early pubs in the parish. Although not mentioned by name, a

The Tamar Inn at Calstock on the right of the picture with the lettering above the door indicating 'Herrings Tamar Hotel' in the early 1900s. Photograph courtesy of the Calstock Archive Trust

1762 newspaper specifically states "near the church". Later newspaper reports mention the *Duke of Cornwall's Arms*, Churchtown. William Burlace [or Borlase][13], who was landlord during the 1760s and 1770s, is listed in the 1766 landholding assession for the parish as holding a house that was formerly a stable near the church, and a new stable. This indicates that the pub had stabling for horses. The Burlace family had land interests throughout the parish, and the inn could have simply been an investment business for them. In a newspaper article of August 1783[SM], Joseph Williams is the landlord, and ten years later in March 1793 [SM] William Almond [Alman] had taken over [his son ran the *Cornish Inn* in Gunnislake].

Tamar Inn

This inn was known as the *Waterman's Arms* [references 1796 – 1819]; *Tamar Inn* [1822 – 26] *Boatsman's Arms* [1827] and the *Tamar Inn* [1850s onwards]. In the Cornwall Industrial Settlements Initiative it states that it is one of the original buildings in Calstock Town[14] dating from the early eighteenth century.[15] It was the venue for the annual manorial Court Baron [1800–1805; 1822–27 and 1844-47].[16]

The first known landlord of the *Waterman's Arms* was Joseph Langman, who records show was also a Quaker. Two years after his death in 1790, his widow, Betsy, remarried to John Cory, who took over as landlord. When he too died in 1802, Betsy ran the pub herself for three years. John Rickard was the licensee for ten years before Thomas Procter became landlord. The Procters are linked with the Metherell brewing family, and John Rickard may be linked with Hannah Rickard later at the *Carpenter's Arms*. There is a gap in the record from the late 1820s until 1841 when Thomas Langman appears as innkeeper in the census; confusingly John Langman is listed from 1844 – 47. It is not clear if this is the same person, nor if either is related to the Joseph Langman of the 1780s. There is more confusion in the middle of the century: John Hutchings is listed as innkeeper in the 1851 census, yet the following year Thomas Rogers[17] is said to be at the inn; with John Hutchings listed again in the Slater's Directory of 1856. John R Ash[18,19] ran the pub for a short time, followed by Samuel Pearse, who in January 1862[WB] was fined for keeping illegal Sunday hours. Edwin Durber ran both the *Tamar Inn* and the *Ashburton Hotel,* but while he was at the *Tamar* he was reprimanded for letting a room for singing and dancing in September 1868[CT]. He seemed to have had an interest in the mines, it was reported in March 1870[GAZ] that Durber of the *Tamar Inn* was busy with the starting of a new engine at South Ward Lead mine. Joseph Prout, followed by his wife Susan, kept the *Tamar* for nearly twenty years from 1878 until 1897, and were succeeded by John Herring. The dangers of the property were highlighted when his son had to be rescued from the river in August 1906 [GAZ]. The twentieth century seems to have been marked by a succession of landlords, but the pub remains an iconic part of Calstock's foreshore.

The Navy and Commercial Hotel, Calstock. Perhaps the lady in Edwardian costume was staying at the hotel?

Photograph courtesy of the Calstock Archive Trust

Navy and Commercial Inn - Commercial Hotel, Calstock

[No longer in operation, Commercial Road opposite the road to Lower Kelly]

This inn was used as the venue for manorial Court Barons [1828-29 and 1848-65]. The early years were stable, but after this it had a series of short-lived landlords in the 1850s, an explanation for which may be that the landlord had his licence suspended in September 1858[WB] "on the grounds of Keeper's misconduct". Joseph Malachi gives his occupation as innkeeper in the parish records of 1818, 1819 and 1820 on the births of his two sons and daughter. Tragically all three died at just a few days old. His sister, Elizabeth, married Thomas Procter of the *Tamar Inn*, and as she appears as landlady of the *Navy and Commercial Inn* in 1828, it is likely that he was the original landlord here. William Mitchell was landlord in 1848, followed a year later by David Mitchell, and in 1851 - 1856 by Hannah Mitchell, widow. She also ran the Steamboat office from the same premises.[DR] A chequered few years followed, during which the inn suffered from a poor reputation, before achieving some stability in the 1860s under Edwin James and Henry Turner Symonds. Hannah Mitchell, who had remained in the village, took over again as landlord in the 1870s. She was succeeded by James Rowe, and John Skinner who was landlord from 1889 – 1897 and also manufactured mineral water. By the early 1900s it was simply known as the *Commercial Hotel*, and seems to have gone out of business by the First World War.

Steam Packet Hotel, Calstock

[No longer a pub, Calstock Quay]

Dated to the early nineteenth century,[20] this three storey building fronted Calstock Quay, but doesn't appear as an inn in the 1839 tithe or 1841 census. There is also confusion because the *Steam Packet Inn* is listed as a separate establishment in the 1861 census, and appears to be at or near the former brewery in Calstock, behind the *Commercial Hotel*. John Hutchings is the first landlord listed at the Hotel in 1851 and again in 1862, but he also ran the *Tamar Inn* in 1856, and another establishment on Fore Street in 1871. In that year the *Steam Packet Hotel* was run by a former Saltash farming couple, John and Betsy Roberts, who were fined for allowing drunkenness in February 1872.[GAZ] [Ten years later John was back in Saltash as a widower]. The 1870s saw Joseph Ward in charge, and the 1880s were dominated by Henry Smale[21], who was succeeded by his son William in 1893. Robert Bowden had already run an inn in Plympton before moving to the *Steam Packet* by 1897, under his ownership in 1906 it is listed as the *Steam Packet Family* and *Commercial Hotel*. Thomas Hill ran it for a long time in the 1920s and 1930s.

Steam Packet Inn

[No longer a pub, behind the former Commercial Hotel above]

This appears to have been a separate establishment behind the *Commercial Hotel* in the 1850s, sixties and seventies; although it is also possible it was simply the pub side of the hotel business.

Devonport Inn, Calstock

[No longer in operation; Baptist Street]

Very little is known about this Inn. It was in operation by 1839 because it is marked on the tithe map next to the Baptist Church, and was originally run by Stephen Spettigue. The death of its landlord; John Langman [also at the *Tamar Inn*] was reported in September 1849[WB]. In the 1850s it may have been run by the Hunn family, and it may have still been in operation in 1871 when John Hutchings appears in the census as a licensed victualler in Fore Street, and the listing places him close to the *Naval and Commercial Hotel* and the *Steam Packet Inn* [not the *Steam Packet Hotel*].

Victoria Inn, Calstock

[No longer in operation; on the western side of The Adit]

This appears to have been established at large premises on The Adit; with quite a large yard which would have been very good as a coaching inn. It appears on the 1839 tithe map and was originally run by Joseph Williams. He was succeeded in 1851 by William Jackman and then by his wife Elizabeth in the early 1860s. Curiously at this time William Jackman himself had moved back to his home village of Lifton, and was describing himself as a "widower" even though Elizabeth was still running the pub and did not die until 1867. A new licence was granted to John Satchell in September 1868.[CT]

New Inn, Calstock

[No longer in operation; number 10 Fore Street]

This building looks very much like all the other commercial premises in Fore Street, and has the appearance of a shop rather than an inn. However in 1852 Robert Brevan was paying the Bowhay family £12 for a year[22] in rent for the *New Inn*. The inn carried on until the 1900s, with John Cock becoming one of the most longstanding landlords in the parish in the 1870s, 1880s and 1890s. He paid a lower rent of £8 a year[23]; and in February 1872 was fined for allowing drunkenness[GAZ,24] James Charles Lawrey took over in the early 1900s, and the pub seems to have closed by the First World War.

Boot Inn

Although the building is much older, and the Boot is reputed to be one of the oldest pubs in Calstock, it first appears as a drinking establishment in Vennings Directory of 1887 when James Searle [bootmaker] was the landlord, the building is said to date from before 1809 in the Cornwall Industrial Settlements Initiative.[25] It clearly gets its name from the other profession of its original landlord. He was succeeded in the early 1900s by his wife Amelia. For a large part of the early twentieth century it was run by James Henry Jane, and his wife Alberta Maude Jane was listed as the landlord in 1939.

Ashburton Hotel, Danescombe

[No longer in operation]

First mentioned in 1861 when it was run by Joseph Wakeham. In September 1871[GAZ] it was described as a building "of three storeys, has large cellars, fourteen or fifteen rooms, on the edge of the Tamar". The licence had lapsed by 1872 when Mr. Bray of Calstock applied for a new one, at the time the East Cornwall mineral railway had just been completed and Mr. Bray submitted that a licence was needed because the area had become a lot busier. The application, in September 1872, was rejected because there were already six public houses in Calstock for a population of 1,100 people, whereas Gunnislake had three public houses for a population of 3000, and it was felt it would be bad for Calstock to have seven pubs.[CT] However, it was running as a pub again by 1878 with Edwin Durber as landlord.[26] Mary Ann Durber carried on after her husband died. It continued on and off as a hotel until the 1990s.

Gunnislake Pubs

Cornish Arms - Commercial Hotel - Bond's Hotel, - Cornish Inn, Gunnislake

The oldest of the Gunnislake pubs, it is first mentioned in 1806 as the venue for manorial Courts Baron until 1821 [from 1816–1821, the name Williams Town was used instead of Gunnislake]. It was marked on the 1815 Davis map as the *Cornish Inn*, and would have been an important coaching inn on the Turnpike road between Tavistock and Callington. Horses were grazed in a field opposite the inn. In 1822 the landlord, William Almond, was sent to debtor's prison in Bodmin, and when he was released he lived at the pub with his relative, Mr. Mitchell, until they fell out in April 1826 when Almond asked him for rent[GAZ]. The pub was sold in November 1826, when it was said to have two dining rooms that could seat 150.[WB] In 1827 it was mentioned in the Act for Improving Roads to and from Callington. It continued to be the venue for important meetings, and the Rural Sanitary Authority met there in 1880. George Adamson, who had previously run the *London Inn* in Dartmouth, was landlord throughout

the 1870s and 1880s, followed by his wife Mary. When Abraham Bond took over in 1893 it was variously known as *Bond's Hotel* and the *Commercial Hotel*. It was clearly seen as a lucrative establishment because in 1910 the Bedford Brewery took it over. Many charabanc trips started from outside the *Cornish Inn* during the 1920s and thirties. It is still in operation as a public house.

Tavistock Inn - Hotel - Arms, Gunnislake

This first appeared as an inn in the 1856 Kelly's Directory, although it may have been a private house before that. Stories that the *Tavistock Inn* was already in existence in 1704 seem unlikely as it doesn't appear on maps or surveys until the 1839 tithe map when it is shown as a T-shaped building. In the 1841 census three families lived in the property. *The Tavistock Inn* was another of the pubs run by the Bowhay family; and the first landlord who appears to have run the pub was paying £2 10s a quarter year in 1857.[27] In 1861 William Broad ran the pub, he had previously been maltster at his parents' pub at Stratton near Bude. James Bolt was landlord in 1871 when his rent had risen to £30 a year,[28] he was also operating as a Granite Merchant.

The *Tavistock Hotel* was mentioned several times at the Brewster Sessions because of concerns about drunkenness. James Bolt lost his licence in September 1872 when magistrates were told "that the house was conducted in a disorderly manner, and that drunken men were seen coming out of it. Bolt was fined in November last for permitting drunkenness in his house, and three of the men that were there at the time were fined for being drink and riotous. Several others had been convicted during the year for being drunk and riotous on the highway after leaving the house". [CT]

The hotel was taken over by William Stephens in 1873 [a different William Stephens to the Latchley farmer so appalled by drunkenness at the beginning of the chapter], but on 8th September 1883 he too had his licence application turned down because "There had been an amazing amount of drunkenness in the neighbourhood. He was sorry to say that during the past year they had had fifty three convictions for drunkenness there, and they had eleven more cases that day, and a great deal of this he believed could be traced to the house in question - the *Tavistock Hotel*".[CT] Stephens managed to overturn the decision, and his wife continued as landlady after his death, until about 1890. John Harris Symons who was landlord from the mid 1890s also calls himself a jobmaster in 1902.

The *Tavistock Arms* was known as a social venue during the twentieth century, for whist drives and functions, as well as becoming celebrated in the village for its Harvest Festival events. The upstairs part which is now used as bedrooms was a "market hall" and an external staircase accessed the room. It was used as a field kitchen and dining room for troops stationed locally during the Second World War.

Hodge's Hotel - Harvey's Hotel - Market Hotel - Johnson's Hotel
[Present day Buccaneer Inn]
This Hotel changed its name with each landlord up until the early 1900s. Joseph

The Rising Sun, Gunnislake, circa 1980

Hodge appeared as an innkeeper in the 1851 census, and in 1856 his establishment was listed as *Hodge's Hotel* [he was also a mine agent as well as an innkeeper]. It appears to have operated as a coaching inn, as in August 1859 "John Harvey returns his sincere thanks for past favours, and begs to acquaint Commercial Travellers and other Gentlemen that they can be accommodated with Horses for Saddle or Harness, Gigs, &c. being an excellent opportunity for persons visiting this locality, or being conveyed to and from Tavistock Railway. The only Hotel where parties can be supplied." John Harvey, who was landlord and also a butcher from 1859 until at least 1889, found himself in front of the bench in 1873 for his own drunken behaviour; being "charged with drunkenness on the highway, on August 10th", he lost his licence.[CT] In 1902 it was *Johnson's Hotel*, run by William Johnson. The 1881 census places this inn on Commercial Street, so it seems to be the forerunner of the *Buccaneer Inn*.

Mason's Arms, Gunnislake
[Building unknown, Under Road]
This beer shop was in Under Road, Gunnislake, close to the Plymouth Brethren chapel, and for most of its existence it was simply listed as a beer retailer, with no name. It was run by Jane Pengelly, and she first appeared as a beer shop keeper in the 1861 census, carrying on until the 1891 census, when the name *"Mason's Arms"* was added. She was a young widow with two small children when she started the business.

Beerhouse, Commercial Street
[Building unknown, in Commercial Street]
This was another beer shop mentioned in the 1861 census as being run by Richard Nichols, and as it was close to several other retail premises, and the Bible Christian Chapel, it was likely to have been at the western end of Commercial Street.

Rising Sun Inn, Calstock Road, Gunnislake
This was first mentioned in the 1871 census, when Peter Daw[s] was listed as a gardener and beer retailer, this pub had few mentions under its name. Objections were raised at the Brewster Sessions in September 1873, claiming that the property was not of sufficient rental value to get a licence "according to the evidence indicated the applicant, for whom Mr. Bridgman appeared, occupied a nine roomed house, for which it was asserted the annual value was in excess of £11 irrespective of licence. An acre and a half of land planted with fruit trees was attached to the house, and the rental of this would be £6 10s, thus bringing the rent to £11 10s. This matter was adjourned for a valuation to be made, but subsequently the application was granted".[CT] Peter Daw[s] ran the pub throughout the 1870s and eighties. One landlord, George Willcocks, had earned enough from his work in America to return to his home area to run the pub in 1901 and 1906.

Bellswood [Bealswood] Inn, Netstakes
[No longer in operation]
In the 1871 census William Jasper was listed as living at this inn, but his job was recorded as a labourer, although in 1873 he appeared in Kelly's Directory as a beer retailer. This could be the

cottage where Temperance George ran her beer shop ten years earlier in 1861.

Bridge Inn - Foresters Arms, Gunnislake
[Building unknown]

The Tamar Brewery at Gunnislake seems to have been on the site by New Bridge that later in the nineteenth century became the Caledonian lodging house. A brew shop owned by William Neblett was listed in this location in the 1839 tithe survey, and it is likely to have been the inn run by Joseph Strick in the 1841 census. The *Bridge Inn* first appears under this name in a November 1846 report of a pigeon shooting match held there and could have been attached to or neighbouring the brewery[WB]. William Bickle [also a butcher], who had been living at Cotehele Quay at the home of John Bickle, maltster in 1841, ran the pub in from at least 1856 until at least 1870 when it was known as the *Forester's Arms*.[29]

Royal Oak, Newbridge
[No longer in operation]

The *Royal Oak* on the Devon side of the river at Newbridge is likely to have been the first inn in the vicinity of Calstock parish to be built on the Turnpike road between Tavistock and Callington dating from around 1769. It is also reputed to be the hotel where Turner stayed when he visited the Tamar Valley in the early 1800s. It appears in the Bowhay Rent Book from 1858 – 1864 with Jacob Harris as landlord and copper miner. It was also the venue for an inquest in September 1874[GAZ] By 1881 Jacob Harris's occupation was listed as farmer, so possibly the inn had closed by then.

Albion Arms, Drakewalls
[Building unknown]

In 1856 and 1862 Richard Doidge was listed as a beer retailer in Drakewalls; but no premises were named. In the census he consistently appears as a mason. In 1861 John Sanders was named as the landlord at the *Albion Arms* [although in the 1863 directory he was innkeeper at the *Cornish Inn*], and in 1871 Catherine Normington was listed as innkeeper at the *Albion Inn*. She lost the licence in October 1871, when it was stated that her husband was in America[CT].

Albaston Pubs

An Albaston pub existed in 1722 with Mr. Colling as innkeeper, but this is likely to be in the lower part of Albaston village, as the area around the current *Queen's Head* hadn't been built up by that time.

Albaston circa 1900, the *Queens Head Hotel* is on the right, with the name of the hotel and the date discreetly engraved in the stonework. CHC Ref: 1998.043.002

Queen's Head, Albaston

The date on the building shown in the postcard on page 61 is 1853, and the Bowhays started collecting rent in 1854 when George Henry Camp paid £20 a year.[30] By the 1871 census he was innkeeper at the *Fountain Inn* in Liskeard. James Mudge, previously landlord at the *Tavistock Inn*, took over in 1860, followed by Henry Northey, when the pub became known as *Northey's Hotel*.[31] It again took the name of its landlord when in 1878 W. Coath was listed as landlord of *Coath's Hotel*, but in the 1881 census Robert Coath was innkeeper at the *Queen's Head*. John Paul who had previously kept an inn at Lower Metherell took over as landlord during 1881, but his licence was endorsed in April 1882 for allowing drunkenness.[WB] Joseph James, who had been a mine agent in Stoke Climsland parish, ran the pub from the 1880s until the early 1900s.

Free Hotel - Butcher's Arms, Albaston
[Building unknown]

It is unlikely that there were more than two pubs in Albaston, so the other references to innkeepers are all likely to have been at the same premises. This was another of the Bowhay pubs, and was likely to have been a large building, because in 1851 and 1854-56 James Gray was paying rent of £40 a year[32] – double the amount for the *Queens Head*. In 1856 and 1862 Thomas Wakem, also a farmer and butcher, was said to be running the *Free Hotel*. [His brother Henry was running the *White Hart* at Chilsworthy and also making a living as a farmer and butcher; and another brother Joseph was running the *Ashburton Hotel*]. In November 1869 Stephen Body of the *Butcher's Arms* was fined for allowing drunkenness and keeping illegal Sunday hours.[GAZ] He was fined again for the same offence in March 1871,[WB] and by the 1871 census had moved to live with his daughter on Newbridge Hill, Gunnislake. In the census he gives his occupation as butcher, or farmer and butcher. Attempts to transfer the licence to Joseph Prout later in 1871 failed; he had previously kept the *Tamar Inn* in Calstock, and the licensing magistrates referred to earlier convictions there.[33]

Metherell, Harrowbarrow, Cotehele
Carpenter's Arms, Metherell

This inn is likely to be one of the oldest in Calstock parish, the *Carpenter's Arms* may well be the inn mentioned as the venue in 1745 for a survey prior to the leasing of some land, with Mrs. White named as the landlady. The 1839 tithe survey listed Samuel Hunn as owner of the building, with Hannah Rickard as the occupier. Samuel Hunn was a carpenter, and his father, grandfather and great grandfather [born 1686] were all carpenters... so it's extremely likely that the pub took its name from this connection. *The Carpenter's Arms* was run by

John Henwood, also a farmer and grocer, in the 1850s and sixties, followed by Samuel Harris in the 1870s and eighties. John Clarke ran it from 1883 until the First World War, and he was succeeded by his son Arnold, who carried on until the Second World War. The inn is still business today.

Lower Metherell Inn *[Building unknown]*
Higher Metherell Inn *[Building unknown]*

These two establishments are also mentioned in directories and censuses and were probably beer shops rather than inns. The *Lower Metherell Inn* seems to have been in business for longer, being run in the 1850s and sixties by John Crook. In December 1876 John Lawrence was fined for being drunk in his own house.[GAZ] There is no mention of this inn after 1878. The *Higher Metherell Inn* is only mentioned in 1861 and 1878.

Country House Inn - Oxford Inn, Cold East/Coombe, Harrowbarrow
[No longer a pub]

This inn regularly appeared in the directories in the mid to late nineteenth century. From the 1850s until 1878 when it was run by Richard Matthew[s], it was known as the *Country House*; and in the 1880s it was run as the *Oxford Arms* by Susan Dawe, in 1884 the licence was renewed despite objections.[GAZ] In 1889 there was a listing for the Harrowbarrow Working Men's Club with the 1891 census listing Cold East Villa as the clubroom. It is not clear whether the club was at the same premises as the inn, but if it is, it could place the pub at Club Cottage at Coombe above Harrowbarrow. This house still carries the name of its former incarnation as a miner's club

Edgecumbe Inn, Cotehele Quay
[No longer a pub, used as a tearoom]

This inn dates from the early nineteenth century.[34] The 1839 tithe survey shows William Bickle at a building at the location of the current *Edgecumbe Inn*; and George Vosper and William Bickle at a building behind this described as a brewhouse. William Bickle was later landlord at the *Bridge Inn*, Gunnislake. William Steed is the first landlord who appears in the record, in the 1841 census. In the 1850s it was run by George Brighton, and in the 1860s and seventies by John Rogers.

St. Ann's Chapel
Calstock Inn - Rifle Corps Inn - Rifle Volunteer, St. Ann's Chapel

A building existed on the site of the current *Rifle Volunteer* on the 1815 Davies map and survey, but the first mention was as the *Calstock Inn*. in the 1827 'Act for Improving Roads to and from Callington'.[35] Samuel Worth appears to have been the first landlord of the *Calstock Inn*, probably called this because it was the first inn encountered in the parish by anyone travelling on the new Turnpike road. Henry Burnman ran the pub for many years in the 1850s and sixties. The name changed after ownership transferred to Henry's son John in 1871. Voluntary Infantry corps were introduced in 1859 because of the perceived threat of a French invasion. Exercises for the local corps were held on Hingston Down, just above St. Ann's Chapel and the pub would have been the nearest watering hole, and must have changed its name because of its best clients. Albert Doidge was another long-standing landlord of the *Rifle Volunteer* from 1910 until close to the outbreak of World War Two.

Sun Inn, St. Ann's Chapel
[No longer a pub, building unknown]
It appears that after handing over the running of the *Rifle Volunteer* to his son, Henry Burnham ran a beer house nearby. In September 1872 his application to renew the licence at the *Sun Inn* was granted following opposition because "the house did not come up to the requirements of the valuation clause. In a parish containing a population of over 2,500, as did Calstock, the annual value should be £11, exclusive of the value of the licence, and if he threw any doubt upon the stated value of the premises it would be in the power of the Bench to adjourn the application for the purpose of a valuation being made. It appeared that two houses had been converted into one, and the applicant's wife stated that the rental was £17 10s".[CT] Henry died in 1876.

Chilsworthy and Latchley
White Hart, Chilsworthy
Henry Wakem, who was also working as a farmer and butcher, was landlord of this inn from 1873 until 1891, although William Slee was listed in addition in 1881 and 1883. In March 1903 When considering whether to renew the licence for the *White Hart* "the Chairman said he had visited it with another magistrate and the only thing they took exception to was the stabling accommodation and sanitary arrangements. Mr. Peter, for the owner, promised that both should be attended to. He handed in a petition in support of renewal. Mr. Foot presented a petition, signed by 180 of the inhabitants, asking that the house be closed. The Chairman remarked that they would soon be receiving petitions to shift the Equator – [laughter]. The sanitary accommodation of the house was very bad, but could easily be remedied". William Gregory was landlord for many years from the First World War until the Second World War.

Public House
Another public house in Chilsworthy was mentioned in the 1871 census but Robert Treloar who was living there gave his occupation as a miner.

Rising Sun
[No longer exists, beside Little Dale Farm]
This inn became notorious because of the fight between two miners in 1860, this is likely to be a pub run next door to the *Latchley Hotel*, now Little Dale Farm, built by the Cocking family. The first edition ordnance survey map shows a house next door [originally owned by Joseph Cocking] as a public house, this building has now been pulled down. The description of the premises given when it came up for let in January 1861 following the fight give a good insight into a typical pub of the time.

> "To be let
> With early possession all that inn or public house called The Rising Sun at Latchley. Premises consists of 2 front parlours, dining room, kitchen, bar, bar parlour, 3 bedrooms, cellar, excellent covered skittle alley, with long room over, coach house, good stabling and every requisite for carrying on a good business. Apply to John Jewells on premises or James Wakem at Chipshop."[CT]

John Jewell was only landlord for a short time until 1860, working as a copper miner before and after this time. In the 1870s, 1880s and 1890s, the *Rising Sun* was run by Thomas Cocking who also owned and ran the *Latchley Hotel*, and who was fined for keeping illegal hours in May 1875.[GAZ]

Latchley Hotel - Latchley Inn, Latchley
[Little Dale Farm]
The *Latchley Hotel* was run by Thomas Cocking, and was more of a miner's hostel than a hotel. It is hard to know whether the *Latchley Inn* was run as a separate establishment or indeed whether it succeeded the *Rising Sun* [above]. Two lean-to cottages were attached to the main building at Little Dale Farm, and it is possible that the inn may have been in one of these. It only appears in 1897 [Albion Jennings] and 1902 [Reuben Copeland]. It probably closed in April 1903 when an appeal against closure was refused.[WB]

Miner's Arms, Latchley
[Possibly the old building next to Kearton Bank; or Ivy Cottage, now demolished]
Very few mentions are made of this inn, but in September 1852 it was the venue for a land survey, so it was probably in a building of some

size.[WB] It lost its licence at the Brewster Sessions in September 1858 because of the innkeeper's misconduct.[WB] In the 1860s Charles Merrel was listed in the 1861 census in Latchley as innkeeper – he could have run the *Miner's Arms*. In 1865 the Philanthropic Society held their annual festival there having "perambulated the village, headed by the Chilsworthy Brass Band, then proceeded to the Wesleyan Chapel". In September 1868 a licence for the *Miner's Arms* was granted to Captain Williams; an objection had been raised by Mr. Cocking proprietor of the *Rising Sun*, but as Captain Williams' house had a higher rateable value than that of Mr. Cocking, the licence was granted.[CT] This indicates a house of some size.

Unless otherwise stated, all references to the inns and pubs are from census returns; and the following directories: Slater's 1852; Kelly's 1856, 1873, 1878, 1883, 1889, 1893, 1897, 1902, 1906, 1910, 1914, 1919, 1923, 1926, 1930, 1935, 1939 ; Harrod's 1862, 1878 ; Venning's 1881, 1887, 1901; Town & Country 1906

Superscript abbreviations
CT   Cornish Times
SM   Sherborne and Yeovil Mercury
GAZ   Royal Cornwall Gazette
WB   West Briton
DR   Street or Postal Directory

1. Minister's Accounts of the Earldom of Cornwall 1296-1297 ed. M.L. Midgley Camden Society 3rd series Vols. LXVI; LXVIII
2. Will of James Adam 1602 Cornwall Record Office AP/A/7
3. Public Record Office SC2 158/115
4. English Heritage Listing LBS 60878
5. Frank Graham, *Old Inns and Taverns of Cornwall*, Newcastle, 1965
6. Court Barons 1822-1865, Calstock Parish Archive
7. 1766 accession from Duchy Record Office
8. An Act for Repairing and Improving Certain Roads Leading to and from Callington in the County of Cornwall, 14th June 1827
9. Callington Roads Act 1764
10. Oral history interview with Gerald Pridham, Calstock Parish Archive
11. Oral history interview with Lewis Pridham, Calstock Parish Archive
12. Oral history interview with Maggie Dodd, Calstock Parish Archive
13. *Sherborne Mercury*, 3rd Aug. 1761, 8th Feb. 1762, 9th Apr. 1764, 15th Mar. 1773 & 16th Mar. 1778
14. Cornwall Historic Services Environmental Report No. 2004R083
15. English Heritage Listing LBS 60878
16. Court Baron records, Calstock Parish Archive
17. *West Briton*, 30th Jan. 1882 Birth of a daughter to J R Ash of the Tamar Inn
18. *West Briton* 10th Dec. 1858, death of wife of J R Ash of Tamar Inn
19. Advertised for sale 8th April 1859
20. English Heritage Listing LBS 60870
21. *West Briton* 22nd Dec. 1890, death of Henry Smale of the Steam Packet Hotel
22. Bowhay Rent Book, Calstock Parish Archive
23. Bowhay Rent Book, Calstock Parish Archive
24. *Royal Cornwall Gazette* 19th Oct. 1911 death of John Cock, 77yrs, late of the New Inn
25. Cornwall Historic Services Environmental Report No. 2004R083
26. *West Briton* 3rd Jan. 1893, Death of Edwin Durbar, 73yrs, of Ashburton Hotel
27. Bowhay Rent Book, Calstock Parish Archive
28. Bowhay Rent Book, Calstock Parish Archive
29. *Royal Cornwall Gazette* 16th Jul. 1870 & 13th Aug. 1870
30. Bowhay Rent Book, Calstock Parish Archive
31. Rural Sanitary Authority meeting, Calstock Parish Archive
32. Bowhay Rent Book, Calstock Parish Archive
33. *Royal Cornwall Gazette* 16th Sep. 1871 & *West Briton* 5th Oct. 1871
34. English Heritage Listing LBS 60840
35. An Act for Repairing and Improving Certain Roads Leading to and from Callington in the County of Cornwall, 14th June 1827

CHAPTER 7

Drinking in St. Dominic

By Alastair Tinto

The *Cornish Arms*, Churchtown

St. Dominick's oldest recorded public house was the *Cornish Arms*, though it no longer exists, having closed down in 1898. However, for at least 150 years, and probably longer, it stood in Churchtown on the site of the present Post Office just across the road from the church and provided drink and society, probably staged games and plays, was a meeting place for the Vestry that ran the parish, was the place where formal notices were lodged, was the venue for auctions and at various times provided lodgings for the homeless. Like most of the landlords in St. Dominick, however, the publicans were never wealthy, usually had other occupations and often lived on the borderlines of poverty.

It is possible that one of the unlicensed ale-houses that was prosecuted in 1633[1] was the *Cornish Arms*. On the other hand John Friendship, whose mother was Alice Lucas, the grand-daughter of the last landlady of *Cornish Arms*, said that the pub had been traced back to 1693 when Wm Smich owned it.[2] It is not clear what the evidence for this is but there is no doubt that in 1702 William Smith was leasing land from the manor of Halton in Churchtown.[3] This may have been the public house.

William and his wife, Elizabeth, had nine children. One suspects that running the *Cornish Arms*, if that was what they did, was not a profitable activity. With a large number of mouths to feed, they found it hard to make ends meet. In 1699 it was "agreed one [on] by the witnesses and the Eightmen[4] of the parish of St. Dominick that John Rich hath taken John Smith the son of William Smith apprentice as if bound by the overseers of the poor of the parish". John, who was ten years old, was their eldest son. The implication is that if his parents had not apprenticed him, the overseers might well have done so and John Rich obviously wanted to ensure that he would not be burdened with another pauper apprentice until the other farmers in the parish had had their turn. Moreover, it lends some support to the notion that William was the landlord of a public house: poor as he may have been the overseers would have been most unlikely to have assisted someone who had at least some means of earning a living. The implication, however, is that William Smith was not much better off than the average pauper.[5]

If William had the *Cornish Arms*, he probably had other land in addition to his tenement at Churchtown. On several occasions between 1701 and 1705 the overseers paid him a shilling or two to supply wood to

paupers in the village. This pattern of the landlord of a public house having additional means of earning a living is a theme that runs throughout the history of pubs in St. Dominick right up to the end of the nineteenth century.

On the 8th October 1701 the overseers paid "Bill Smith for Henders wife 3s". This was Phebe Hender, whose sixty-eight year old husband, William, had just died. Phebe came from Lanreath. It looks as if when Phebe was widowed in 1701 the overseers had to put her up at the *Cornish Arms* for a week or whilst some more permanent accommodation was sorted out. We will see that the *Cornish Arms* was regularly used by the overseers to accommodate poor people.

William died in 1742 but by that time the pub had been taken over by Samuel Congdon. Samuel had moved to St. Dominick when he married a local girl in 1734 though we don't know where he originated from. Initially they lived on a small seven acre small-holding in Ashton.[6] He may have been a tailor because in 1740 the overseers paid him "8d for making clothing of the poor". However, a year later he was paid by the overseers "for gallon of brandy at Griffin Congdon's funeral".[7] How touching it is that the parish would even go so far as to provide brandy for one of their pauper's funerals! We know for sure that he was the landlord by April 1745 because the 'Sherborne Mercury' records a survey, or auction, of wood being held "in the house of Samuel Congdon, innkeeper, in St. Dominick Churchtown". For several years in the 1750s, after he had given up the pub, Samuel received various handouts from the overseers.

In April 1749 there was another advert in the 'Sherborne Mercury' for a survey for a number of leases in St. Dominick owned by Thomas Scawen that was to be held "at the house of Mr. Thomas Potts, Innkeeper, in the parish of St. Dominick". It looks, therefore, as if Potts had taken over the pub from Samuel Congdon. There is no record, other than this advertisement, of a Thomas Potts in St. Dominick. However, by 1748 John and Elizabeth Potts had moved into the village where they had a number of children. Moreover in 1748 Elizabeth was paid by the overseers for supplying a gallon of brandy for the funerals of two paupers.[8] This suggests that by then they were innkeepers. It looks possible, therefore, that the 'Mercury' may have got John's name muddled and called him Thomas by mistake. We do not know how long Potts stayed at the *Cornish Arms* but it can't have been very long because in

1753 Elizabeth started to receive a weekly dole from the overseers of three shillings a week for her children. The fact Samuel Congdon and John and Elizabeth Potts ended up on the parish not many years after they had been running the pub reinforces the view that being a landlord of a village public house in this period was not a very profitable occupation.

There is a gap of nearly forty years in our knowledge of the *Cornish Arms* until two marriages, one in 1787 when William Hawkins married Mary Crober and the other when Robert Lucas also married a Mary Crober, a widow, in April 1789. In the marriage registers William is referred to as an inn holder and Robert as an innkeeper. What are we to make of the marriages of these two innkeepers and their Mary Crobers? It is unlikely that they are the same Mary because William and Mary had two children, the last of whom was baptised in January 1790, over eight months after Robert married his Mary Crober. However, the innkeeping link and their names, which are otherwise unknown in St. Dominick, suggest that the two Marys were related, sisters-in-law, perhaps. We have no evidence that William's inn was the *Cornish Arms* but it is possible that he was running the *Cornish Arms* when he got married but that Robert, through the family link between their two wives, took it over soon after. The Lucas family went back a long way in St. Dominick. His father and grand-father, both Roberts, were the tenants of Radland Mill, which is half a mile from the *Cornish Arms* at the bottom of Pepper's Hill.[9] Robert, his son and his grandson ran the *Cornish Arms* for over a century until it was knocked down and replaced by the post office in 1902.

In 1791 Robert took out a lease from the Earl of Mount Edgcumbe for some dwelling houses, an orchard and a meadow in Churchtown known as the Playing Place. This is the only reference there is to a playing place in St. Dominick, although playing places, *plen an gwary* in Cornish, were common throughout Cornwall. They were outdoor theatres where small strolling companies of actors would perform morality or miracle plays. Moreover, they were often found in inn-yards.[10] Richard Carew, Cornwall's earliest historian, wrote in 1602 of the Gwary miracle, or miracle play, that "for representing it they raise an earthen Amphitheatre, in some open field, having the Diameter of his enclosed playne some 40 or 50 foot.[11] The Country people flock from all sides, many miles off, to heare and see it: for they have therein, devils and devices, to delight as well the eye as the ear".[12] Perhaps events such as these happened at the *Cornish Arms*.

We have no idea when the pub was built but John Friendship says that it was right on the roadside. All that is left of the pub now is the slate mounting stone and slate step by the letter box which is where the pub door was originally. Its roof was part slate and part thatch. At the end of the nineteenth century it

was often called the Black Hole of Calcutta because it was so dim inside. There was a yard & stables at the back.[13]

Robert's lease on Playing Place was a typical Cornish ninety-nine year lease based on a number of lives. Usually there were three lives, although Robert's 1791 lease only had two, those of himself and of his son, Robert. The tenant would put his own life and perhaps that of his wife and youngest son on the lease. Each time one of the names on the lease died a "fine" or heriot was paid to the landlord. When the last of the names died the lease expired. The idea was that the tenancy would be safeguarded for the life of the tenant himself, of his widow and of the son that might inherit it. The 1791 Playing Place lease contained all the terms of a tenancy that would be found in much older mediaeval leases. The heriot was £1 or his best beast, a reference to the earlier practice in which the landlord claimed the best beast in a tenant's stock each time one of the names in the lease died. In addition to the rent of £2 a year, Robert had to attend the manorial court. He was also required to grind his corn at the ancient manorial mill at Mordon, now known as Cotehele Mill, thereby ensuring the lord an extra source of income.

As with William Smith, the *Cornish Arms* was not Robert's only source of income.[13] He also leased from the Earl of Mount Edgcumbe an eight acre smallholding at Vernigo called Lark's Tenement.[14]

We saw how the overseers of the poor used the *Cornish Arms* as a lodging house for their paupers when William Smith was the landlord. The Lucases also took in boarders paid for by the overseers. In 1790 Robert was paid 7s 9½d for meat and lodging for Elizabeth Knight, a young single mother who had just started to receive assistance from the overseers. It may be that when she first arrived, moved on perhaps by another parish because she really belonged to St. Dominick, the overseers needed to lodge her in the *Cornish Arms* until they found something more permanent, for shortly after this they paid 10s 5½d for household goods and rug, which suggests that she was then setting up in a house.

The Lucases also took in lodgers on a more permanent basis. In 1795 Robert was paid 12s for lodging Joseph Hambley. Joseph was a bit of a nuisance to the St. Dominick overseers who were constantly trying to get rid of him. In 1792 they paid him one guinea "to March off and never to come no more". A year later they paid him another £1 or so "when he went away" and soon after Lucas took him on in 1795 they paid "10s 6d on quitting the parish".

However, to no avail. In 1796, when Hambley was in his sixties, they accepted responsibility and for forty weeks paid him a pension of 2s a week and paid £6 4s to "Mr. Lucas for lodging him and cleaning him". Lucas, who was obviously prepared to offer more than just lodging, carried on caring for him for the next five years until Joseph died in 1801. He was paid 2s a week plus 9d "for cleaning him", a reminder that care in the community was an essential element in the care of the elderly well over two hundred years ago. Ten years later in 1802 Lucas charged 10s 4d "for meat and lodging" Cattern Cocking, another single mother, and her two year old illegitimate son, James, whose father was a Harrowbarrow man called James Pine whom the overseers hounded for the next four or five years for his maintenance.

Robert Lucas's caring role also extended to child care. Between 1800 and 1803 he looked after John Hawkins for 2s a week until he was bound apprentice and in 1801 Mary, Robert's wife, was paid 3s "for 2 pair stockings for Mary Hawkins girl". It is very likely that John and Mary Hawkins were the children of Mary Crober who had married William Hawkins in 1787 and who we speculated earlier may have been Mary Lucas's sister-in-law. We see how networks of kinship meshed with the Poor Law to ensure that the parish looked after its own. If there was harshness in the way that the overseers tried to get rid of people they did not consider part of their community, like John Hambly, for instance, those that they accepted were looked after and provided for humanely in ways supportive to community and family.

In 1813 Robert began planning for the future. In July of that year he assigned the lease of the inn to his eldest son, Robert Lucas junior, retaining a life interest for himself.[15] Mary, his wife, may have been ill because a few months later she died at the age of sixty-one. Although he was quite a bit younger than his wife, he must have pondered his own mortality. As his eldest son was in his twenties, this was an ideal time to begin the process of handing over the running of the *Cornish Arms*.

Round about this time Robert junior married a St. Dominick girl called Mary Ann and started a family. Robert and Mary Ann's first child, William Nanscawen Lucas, was born in 1815. There followed seven more children between then and 1829, all of whom were boys.

In 1817 Robert senior surrendered the 1791 lease and took out a new one on the lives of himself, his son, Robert, and Robert's new wife, Mary Ann. They had obviously decided to get her name on the lease in case anything happened to her husband. It looks as if Robert junior was now very much in partnership with his father, running the *Cornish Arms*.

It is clear from the baptismal registers that Robert, like his father and most of the earlier landlords, did not rely solely on the *Cornish Arms* for his income. On the entries for most of his children he is referred to as "victualler and farmer". Indeed on William's entry he is simply known as a farmer. It is probable that he farmed the same eight acre holding that his father had at Vernigo.

Sometime at the end of the 1820s the Lucases seem to have ceased for a time to be the landlords of the *Cornish Arms* but they retained the lease. When his youngest son, Richard, was born in 1829 the baptismal record refers to Robert merely as a labourer, suggesting not only that he had come down in the world but that he was no longer running the public house. Moreover, the churchwardens' rate books show that in 1830 George Trewin paid a rate of 3d for the "Publick House". By 1832 John Spear had obviously taken over as he too paid 3d rates, the rate book clearly stating that it was for the *Cornish Arms*. He stayed there for the next ten years.

Around the same time, in 1832, Robert senior, using the lease on the *Cornish Arms* as collateral, borrowed £80 on a mortgage from Charles Smith, a cordwainer [shoemaker] from St. Ive. It seems that big changes of some kind or another were happening in the Lucas family.

George Trewin was the landlord of the *Cornish Arms* for no more than a year or two between 1830 and 1832. He was born in Devonport in about 1804[CS]. When he first came to St. Dominick around 1830 he was a butcher based in Churchtown[16] and may have combined butchery with running the pub. In 1832 he gave up the pub to take over the tenancies of farms at Burraton and Morden.[17]

We know even less about John Spear than we do about George Trewin. He was a Cornishman and took over the *Cornish Arms* in his mid-twenties[CS]. He may have moved to St. Dominick to run the pub because the earliest record of him is the entry in the baptismal register on the birth of his eldest daughter, Mary, in November 1832 when he was referred to as victualler of Churchtown. Like William Smith and Robert Lucas before him he took in lodgers. In 1836 "the Vestry decided on allowing John Bennett a little boy living with Mr. Spear innkeeper a suit of clothes".[18] He was still at the *Cornish Arms* in 1841.

By the end of John Spear's tenure we can see the impact of the 1830 Beer Act: the *Cornish Arms* was facing competition from two other public houses in the area. In 1839 John Diamond was paying 3d rates on some "cottages and beer shop" at Cross and in 1841 Stephen Martin was the landlord of the *Maltster's Arms* on Halton Quay[CS]. Not long after that in 1847 John Poad, a mason from Ashton, complained that his rates for his beer shop, which was probably in Tipwell, were too high.[19] There is no evidence of how this competition affected the *Cornish*. Poad's beer shop was short lived but the *Maltster's Arms* was still operating in the 1860s. Dimond's beer shop at Cross may have turned into the *Butcher's Arms*. It is now called the *Who'd Have Thought It* and is St. Dominick's only surviving public house.

Robert Lucas senior died intestate in 1838[20] and only a year later Robert junior renegotiated the lease in much the same way that his father had done when he was about to take over the pub. By 1839 Robert junior's eldest boy, William Nanscawen Lucas, was twenty-four and in the new lease of that year Robert had his son included as one of the names. It looks very much as if he was lining him up to be the next landlord. In effect the new lease added William as one of the names so that if Robert and Mary Ann, William's parents, died he would still have the lease.[21] At one point in his life William appears to have been a schoolmaster of some kind.[22] Whether this was before his *Cornish Arms* days we do not know. However, what is certain is that by 1842 William had taken over at the pub from John Spear.

Once he settled in as landlord, William was active in helping to run the affairs of the parish. He was a Constable in 1849, an Overseer for the Poor in 1851, Surveyor of Highways in 1853 and a member of the Vestry in 1854.[23] In the 1860s, as parish clerk, he was regularly used to witness marriages in the parish church[PR]. In 1869 he was appointed Collector of Rates for the parish for an annual fee of £11.[24] and in 1871 he was an enumerator for the census. For most of the time from then until his death in 1883 William lived at the pub and the *Cornish Arms* seems to have been his main livelihood. However, like his father and grand-father before him, he also had farming interests. He owned thirty-three acres at Gooseford which he rented out.

In 1860 there was an extensive refurbishment of the pub which cost over £4. It included a new wall for the Kayle Ally which would have been a bowling alley. The upgrading may have been to get it ready for tenanting for in the early 1860s William got tenants in at the pub and farmed full time on the church land that he rented just up the road at Trehill.[25]

Benjamin Bond, a former miner from St. Dominick, was his first tenant, running the pub from 1860 to 1861.[26] Samuel Worth, another St. Dominick man, who had been running a grocer's shop just round the corner in Baber, took over from Bond.[CS] Worth seems to have been pretty useless as a landlord and was constantly falling foul of the law. In January

1863 he was fined 15s plus costs "for keeping open his house after proper hours". A year later he was summoned by Inspector Marshall for permitting drunkenness and other disorderly conduct in his house the night of the last fair. Sergeant Rosevear and PC Downing were called and proved that they visited the house several times during the night and found a number of men drunk and wanting to fight, and that the house was not cleared until between four and five in the morning". In September 1867 his licence was refused because of three previous convictions. However, in November that year he was still at the *Cornish* because at Callington Petty Sessions he was fined £1 and costs "for keeping for keeping his house open for the sale of intoxicating liquors in the parish of St. Dominick after 10 o'clock".[27]

The letting out of the *Cornish Arms* coincided with a renegotiation of the lease between William and his

The Cornish Arms, probably taken in the early 1890's. The licensing board over the door names Mary Lucas.

father, Robert, who was now seventy years of age. Robert seems to have sunk on hard times. A new lease of 1860 gave him the lowly status of labourer and referred to a loan of £200 which William had made him. This debt was cancelled by the purchase of the lease by William from Robert for £200. There was a covenant that William would provide his father

with "good and sufficient lodging and attendance in William's house for life". Robert's care in his old age was secured.[28] He died aged seventy-nine in 1869.[29]

William himself also seems to have needed money. A deed of 1861 refers to a loan that Charles Smith of Menheniot had made him in 1857. We do not know how much the loan was but the repayment of it was very interesting. William took out an insurance policy on his life with the Scottish Equitable Life Assurance Society which would pay out £100 to Smith on William's death. Smith paid the annual premium of £3 12s. William also owed Samuel Lang, a merchant from Cotehele Quay, £56. In 1861 Lang lent William another £177 which was secured by a mortgage on the *Cornish Arms* and another life policy for £100 which along with Smith's policy was assigned to Lang. It looks as if William paid off Smith with some of the money Lang had lent him.[30]

Two years later Samuel Lang wanted his money back so Thomas Martin, the brewer of Towell Farm, paid Lang his £233. Furthermore for £5 and the assignment of the two insurance policies he acquired the lease of the *Cornish Arms*. William was now a tenant of Martin.[31] There is no evidence that Martin had anything much to do with the *Cornish Arms* other than as the leaseholder but it would fit well with his brewing business that he had the pub as an outlet for his beer.

When Natalie Allen was writing her excellent book on St. Dominick, 'A Stitch In Time', she was lucky enough to see an account book, now lost, for the *Cornish Arms* dating back to 1861 which was in the possession of John Friendship, William's great-grandson. A pint of gin cost 2s 5½ d, three glasses of beer 4½ d and a tot of brandy 2d.[32]

Pubs then, as they do today, clearly played an important part in the life of the parish and not just for the hardened drinkers. Les Babb recalled that the bell ringers went to the stables at the back of the pub with a barrel of beer after they had rung for a wedding or other special occasions, the pub being just across the road from the church.[33] The annual St. Dominick fair which was held on the first Thursday after 12th May was always held outside the *Cornish Arms*. It moved to the *Butcher's Arms* when the *Cornish* was demolished. It continued here until after the end of the First World War.[34]

The *Cornish Arms* played a significant role in facilitating the running of parish affairs. It provided a place for meetings. In 1841, for example, the Tithe Commissioners held their first meeting to consider the commutation of tithes in St. Dominick in the pub. It was also a kind of post box for important parish matters. In 1854, for instance, the Vestry instructed the way wardens to draw up a contract to be lodged at the *Cornish Inn* for those wanting to repair the roads in the parish.[35]

When William died in 1883 his widow, Mary Ann Lucas, kept the pub going[DR] with assistance from her grand-daughter, Alice, who had been brought up by her grandparents since she was a little girl[CS]. In January 1898 Mary, who by then was eighty-seven, was summoned to the Callington Brewsters Sessions on a charge of supplying beer to a child under the age of thirteen. A policeman had found George Cradick, whose father had the farm up the road at Trehill[CS], "with a glass of beer before him". Mrs. Lucas did not appear in court but her thirty year old grand-daughter, who by now was managing the business, admitted serving the boy "being ignorant that she was doing wrong". She was surely being disingenuous but this does nonetheless suggest that under-age drinking was a common phenomenon in the *Cornish Arms*. They were fined ten shillings and had to pay costs[CT].

The board that was over the door to the Cornish Arms, shown in the previous photograph.

Despite the underage drinking, the *Cornish Arms* under Mary Ann Lucas maintained good order. In September 1898[CT] the Callington Brewsters Sessions received a report summarising their activity over the previous year. Their area covered a population of 16,079 in which there were forty licensed premises of which the *Cornish Arms* was one, which meant one pub to every four hundred inhabitants. There had been forty-seven prosecutions for drunkenness, mainly in Callington, Calstock which had twenty cases, and Gunnislake. There were no prosecutions in St. Dominick. Trippers from Plymouth were held partly to explain the numbers in Calstock!

Mary died on 28 August 1898[36] a month before this report and with her death the *Cornish Arms* came to an end. At Callington Petty Sessions in October

1898[CT] it was reported that the Earl of Mount Edgcumbe, the owner of the property, "refused to allow the house any longer to be used as an inn". Alice, Mary's grand-daughter, married a St. Dominick labourer called William Friendship in July 1899[PR]. The pub was demolished and the present Post Office and house were built on the site. The new Post Office was opened in 1902 by a St. Dominick shopkeeper called James Rabbage who moved to the premises from his shop in Under Lane.[37]

Thomas Dimond's Beer Shop, Cross

In 1839 Thomas Dimond paid 3d rates for some cottagers and a beer shop at Cross.[38] He was a carpenter in his late forties whose family had been in St. Dominick for several generations. He had lived at Cross since 1829 and remained there until his death in 1863. It is probable that he combined running the beer shop with his trade as a carpenter because in the 1841 census he was recorded as a carpenter and in 1851 as a wheelwright. On the other hand, when his son, John, got married in 1847 Thomas's occupation was given as innkeeper.

The *Butcher's Arms,* also known as the *Sheffield*, and now called *The Who'd Have Thought It*, Cross

It is possible that Thomas Dimond's beer shop at Cross was the start of the *Butcher's Arms*, now called the *Who'd Have Thought It*, which stands more or less at Cross. However, Leonard Hughes, interviewed by Natalie Allen in the 1980s, knew about the beer shop at Cross but said that the Cousens family opened the *Butchers' Arms* in the 1850s.[39]

In fact the pub was built on Mount Edgcumbe land in the 1840s by John Wall, the landlord of the *Three Crowns* on the Barbican in Plymouth who was married to a St. Dominick girl.[40] Wall may have installed the Cousens as his tenants. Drew Potter, who ran the pub at the end of the twentieth century, believes that what is now one public house was originally small three cottages.

John Cousens was a carpenter from Devonport. In 1845 he married Mary Ann Herring, the daughter of a St. Dominick farmer, and moved to St. Dominick. By 1851 they were innkeepers at Sheffield Cottages, soon to be known as the *Butchers' Arms*. John kept on his trade as a carpenter combining it with the running of the pub for the next forty years until his death at the age of sixty-nine in 1892. Mary Ann continued at the pub as landlady until she died in 1906. Indeed, Mary Ann was a key figure in the management of the public house throughout their years together. A newspaper report, for example, in March 1858[GAZ] refers to "Mary Ann Cozens, who keeps the *Butchers' Arms*".

Whether or not the *Butchers' Arms* started as a beer shop, it is clear that very soon it had become a public house providing food as well as drink. On the 8th November 1859, for instance, John Cousens paid Richard Cradick 15s for 27½ lbs of pork.[41]

In the winter of 1857 the *Butchers' Arms* was involved in a murder case. Indeed, Mary Ann Cousens was called to give evidence. The case involved a farm worker called William Nattle who lived about a quarter of a mile up the road from the pub with his widowed mother. One Saturday William went on a drinking spree, starting in Mary Ann's pub in the morning with a pint. He then moved on and obviously had a skinful because he came back to the *Butchers' Arms* at about 4.15 in the afternoon for another pint. Mary Ann refused him because she thought he had had enough. He staggered home where later that evening his mother was found lying by the fire, bruised behind the ear. William had a reputation as a bit of a drunkard and had often been heard threatening her when he was the worse for drink. He was charged with his mother's murder but there was not sufficient evidence for a conviction and the jury at the Assizes found him not guilty.[42]

A hunt meet at the Butchers Arms, probably circa 1930-1940. This was before the rendering was removed. Photograph courtesy of D & L Potter

The pub's official name was the *Butchers' Arms*. It is referred to as such in trades directories, newspaper reports and magistrates courts. However, for most of its history, until it was renamed the *Who'd Have Thought It* in the 1960s, it has been known colloquially at the *Sheffield*. Leonard Hughes, whose mother-in-law had worked there under the Cousens at the end of the nineteenth century, told Natalie Allen that "cutlery and Sheffield steelware was sold there at some period and that's how it got the name *Sheffield*".[43] This story presumably relates back to the 1830s when William Westlake, a blacksmith and ironmonger, moved into a newly built cottage and shop at Cross called Sheffield Cottages where he plied his trade.[44]

When Mary Ann died Jack Rogers, an ex-policeman from London who had been brought up in St. Dominick, took over the lease and ran the pub with his daughter, Flo. Henry Rickard gives some idea of what a pub was like at the turn of the century. He told Natalie Allen that "it was a rough place at that time, just a bar and another small room". There were no lavatories, just an old shed at the back. Beer was 1d a pint and "twas an awful job when it went up to 2d". Doris Webber confirms this impression. She says the pub "was rather rough in the old days". When she was a child at the beginning of the twentieth century St. Dominick Fair was held on the green outside the pub. Stalls were set up where sweets, ornaments and toys were sold. "Many years before", so her father said, cattle were sold on the green. Occasionally pony racing was held in a nearby field. The Coronation celebrations in 1910 were held there. The pub continued to be a social focal point.

Rogers ran the "Sheffield" for many years. His wife, Elizabeth, died in 1931[45] but he carried on until 1939 when Frances Spark of the *Halfway House* in Polbathic bought the freehold from the Earl of Mount Edgcumbe for £2300.[46] During the nineteen forties and fifties the pub went through a number of owners including at least two other women.[47].

In 1962 the pub was bought by Eddie and Lily Potter. At that time there were three licensed rooms on the ground floor serviced by a single bar. Ed Potter was an experienced publican and he and his wife quickly turned the pub into a thriving business. They immediately renamed it *The Who'd Have Thought It* because they did not want it confused with the *Butcher's Arms* in St. Ive. Gradually they extended the pub, building a new bar and creating restaurant space. Over the years their son, Drew, became more involved with the pub, eventually taking over from his parents. He retired in 2003 and the pub is now owned by St. Austell Breweries.

The Maltster's Arms, Halton Quay

In 1841 another pub appeared, the *Maltster's Arms*. It was probably at Halton Quay where James Bennett was running a pub of the same name in the 1850's.

The Quay was a busy place and must have been an ideal location for a pub. G P Hearder in his 'Guide To The River Tamar' [1841] describes it as a place "whence marketable commodities are shipped for the towns of Devonport and Plymouth; and limestone, manure, coal etc are received in return. A large building stands on the bank of the river on the quay erected as a granary. Lime kilns, a few cottages and a small ale-house, with a few market boats complete the scene".

This pub was run by Stephen Martin, a man with deep roots in St. Dominick who had worked on the land before this, sometimes as a labourer and sometimes with a bit of land of his own. He lived in Bohetheric. How long he ran the pub for is not known. Certainly in 1845 when his son, Richard, married he was still an innkeeper. However, in 1851 he was working again as a labourer.[cs]

In 1856 James Grills Bennett, a St. Dominick man, was running the pub. We know that he was still there in 1863 because W J May, an auctioneer from Hatt, held an auction there of some woodland at Halton Barton, just up the road from the pub.[48]

The next landlord we have a record of at the *Maltster's Arms* was James's very much younger brother, Edmund, a miner. He probably took over the pub from his brother and like many landlords seems to have run the pub in conjunction with his normal occupation. It may have been Edmund's mining background that gave the *Maltster's Arms* a reputation for after hours drinking. In 1867 his application for a licence was adjourned. Two years later he was fined 20s and costs for drawing beer during illegal hours on a Sunday. And in 1876 the police requested the magistrates for another adjournment of his licence application "on the ground of the house being unfit for a public house". This evidence supports Sarah Mason's memory, recorded by Natalie Allen, of a pub at Halton Quay that "was open all hours. On Sunday mornings it would be full of customers. The landlady would call out 'Who wants a piece of orange pasty?' which were big, full of swede, turnips and lots of salt. The salt in the pasties made the men thirsty and kept them there all afternoon". The inn, she said, had a thatched roof. After the 1876 case we hear no more of Edmund as a landlord and by 1881 he was living in Churchtown and working as a farm labourer.[49]

Tamar Inn, Bohetherick

Kelly's Directory of 1856 lists Thomas Hawton as the innkeeper at the *Tamar Inn*. There was at this time living in St. Dominick a thirty year old labourer of the same name who may have been the landlord of the *Tamar Inn*. In 1861 Thomas is listed as a lead miner living in Smeaton.

In 1859 an innkeeper of St. Dominick called John Normington was summoned before the Callington

Petty Sessions for keeping his house open for the sale of liquor on the 11th November beyond the time allowed by law. P C King visited the house on that day and found eight persons drinking in the back room. He was fined £1 and costs. A few months later he was back at the Petty Sessions "for keeping his house open for the sale of excisable liquor at 1.50 am". Mr. Chilcott, Normington's solicitor, said that as four of the men slept there he was not liable. But the policeman said that he knew that two of them lived in the same village. Magistrates overruled the objection and he was fined £2 plus costs. We have no name for this pub nor any indication of whereabouts in St. Dominick it was. However, it seems very likely that he took over from Thomas Hawton at the *Tamar Inn*. [50]

In 1861, according to the census, Samuel Pearce from Tywardreath was running the *Tamar Inn* in Bohetherick. We know nothing else about him but it may be that John Normington gave up the pub soon after the court case and that he took over. Harrison's Directory of 1862 has Thomas Hawton and William Pearce at the *Tamar Inn*. Should William Pearce perhaps be Samuel? And does this suggest that there were two *Tamar Inns* in St. Dominick? Or were Pearce and Hawton jointly landlords there? And did Hawton return there after his stint of lead mining?

Natalie Allen says that her grandmother's aunt and uncle, Mr. and Mrs. Hockaday, were the last landlords of a pub next to Tamar View in Bohetherick. Since her grandmother was born around 1860 this would date the Hockadays very appropriately for the *Tamar Inn* after William Pearce and Thomas Hawton. It seems very likely that a pub next to Tamar View might be called the *Tamar Inn*.

Superscript abbreviations
CT   Cornish Times
GAZ   Royal Cornwall Gazette
DR   Street or Postal Directory
1. Certificates of Justices of the Peace, 6th May 1631, SP/16/190/37 and 8th May 1633, SP16/284/61. See also Chapter 2
2. Natalie Allen, *A Stitch in Time*, N. R. Allen, Saltash, 1984 p.33
3. Indenture of Sale of Parts of Halton Manor, Cornwall Record Office, [CRO] ME116
4. The Eightmen of the parish made up the Vestry which governed parish affairs. Whenever one of them died, he was replaced by another, nominated alternately by the Rector and by the Eightmen themselves.
5. The accounts of the Overseers of the Poor for St. Dominick are at Cornwall Record Office, DDP/50/12/1-5
6. Manor of Ashton Barton, Extent, 1735, CRO DDR 3785/2/3
7. St. Dominick Overseer Accounts CRO DDP/50/12/3
8. St. Dominick Overseer Accounts CRO DDP/50/12/3
9. Manor of Ashton Barton, Rental 1740, CRO DDR 3762/2
10. R Moreton Nance, *The Plen an Gwary or Cornish Playing-Place*, Journal of the Royal Institute of Cornwall, Vol. XXIV Part 3 – 1935, Journal No.82, p.190
11. 40 to 50 feet is approximately 12 to 15 metres
12. Richard Carew, *The Survey of Cornwall*, London, 1602, f72
13. Allen, p.33
14. Indenture, lease on Playing Place Churchtown, formerly in a collection of documents relating to Towell Farm but now at the CRO
15. Land Tax c.1798/99, CRO AD103/228; Tithe Map and Schedule of St. Dominick, c.1842 National Archives, 1 IR29/6/43 CAPS/A 02048, p.6
16. Indenture. Mortgage of Cornish Arms from Robert Lucas to Charles Smith, 1840, CRO
17. Baptismal record of his son, William, 12th Dec. 1830
18. Churchwarden's Accounts, CRO, DDP/50/5; 1842 tithe schedule
19. Select Vestry Minutes, CRO, DDP/50/8/1
20. St. Dominick Vestry Minutes, CRO, DDP/50/8/1 15th Dec. 1847
21. Reassignment of lease 1860, CRO
22. Indenture. Lease on Cornish Arms 1839 from Richard Earl of Mount Edgcumbe to Robert Lucas, CRO
23. Poor Law Board's [PLB] Correspondence Liskeard Union, National Archive, MH12/1437
24. Select Vestry Minutes, CRO, DDP/50/8/1
25. PLB Correspondence, as note 23 above
26. Tithe Schedule 1842. Assignment of lease 1860, CRO, Allen p.41
27. Assignment of lease 1860, CRO; Indenture, Assignment of Cornish Arms by way of mortgage from William Nanscawen Lucas to Samuel Lang, 1861, CRO
28. *Cornish Times* 10th Jan. 1863 & 11th June 1864; *Royal Cornwall Gazette* 12th Sep. & 14th Nov. 1867
29. Assignment of Lease, 1860, CRO
30. Memorial stone in St. Dominick churchyard
31. Indenture. Assignment of Cornish Arms 1861, as note 27 above
32. Indenture, transfer of mortgage as note 27 above
33. Allen, p.35
34. Allen, p.46
35. Allen, p.55
36. *West Briton* 1st Jan. 1841. Vestry Minutes CRO, DDP/50/8/1 27th Mar. 1853
37. Monumental Inscriptions, Cornwall Family History Society
38. Allen, p.47
39. St. Dominick Churchwarden's Accounts, CRO DDP/50/5
40. St. Dominick Churchwarden's Accounts, CRO DDP/50/5 p.68
41. This information comes from notes made by the late Arthur Rabbage, the St. Dominick historian, supplied to the author by his daughter, Mrs. Kay Pearce. Unfortunately he did not leave a reference for the source of the information
42. Notebook of Richard Cradick, c.1850-1874, in the possession of William Bolt of Bristol
43. *Royal Cornwall Gazette* 4th Dec. 1857, 25th Dec. 1857, 1st Jan. 1858 & 26th Mar. 1858
44. Allen, p.55
45. Churchwarden's Accounts and 1841 census
46. Allen p.59 and *Kelly's Directory* 1910-1939
47. Abstract of title of Mrs. Frances Spark, 1943, in the possession of Mr. D Potter
48. Schedule attached to Conveyance of 13th July 1961 between George Francis Herbert and Ernest James Reep in the possession of Drew Potter
49. *Kelly's Directory* 1856, *Cornish Times* 21st Feb. 1863
50. *Royal Cornwall Gazette* 12th Dec. 1887, *West Briton* 13th May 1869 and 11th Sep. 1878, Allen p.93, Census 1871 & 1881
51. *Cornish Times* 10th Dec. 1859, *Royal Cornwall Gazette* 13th Apr. 1850

CHAPTER 8
Village Inn

By Miranda Lawrance Owen and Lynda Mudle-Small

The picturesque public house in the centre of a village adjacent to an ancient church is quintessentially English. It is the image many holiday brochures promote and expatriates dream off, as there is nothing quite like it in any other country.

Cornwall has it fair share of village inns adjacent to the parish church and around Callington they belong, in most cases to the smaller parishes. Pillaton and St. Mellion are classic examples, as well as the old village of St. Ive.

The Church and the Inn.
As has been demonstrated in the first chapter the church was originally closely linked with the local alehouse. A very detailed picture of the importance of church houses and church ales comes from the parish of Morebath, in Devon.[1] It is clear that "the church house was the centre of conviviality and shared feasting in the parish, the place where the parish sat down together to drink and unwind".[2] Morebath was a small, poor and relatively remote parish, probably not dissimilar from some of the parishes around Callington such as Pillaton or St. Dominic. If church ales formed such an important part of the life of Morebath, it seems likely that they would have been just as important in this area and that there would have been church houses connected with many if not all of the pre sixteenth century churches in the Callington area. One can speculate that today's pubs in St. Ive, Pillaton or St. Mellion may have originally been the church houses although no evidence has so far been found to support this

A Meeting Place
As the church gradually divorced itself from alcoholic excesses and drunken feasting, one of the unintended consequences was the lessening of the part played by the Church in community life. Once churches were no longer the centre of communal celebrations, this made room for alehouses and inns to assume a wider role than that of mere drinking houses or hospitality for travellers. They became the common gathering place, the focus for news and gossip and the new place for communal celebration of events such as weddings. As time went on they became centres of "local administration in politics, the places where feasts and banquets were held and where the county and urban gentry met for social and intellectual activities ranging from cockfighting to lectures and debates".[3]

Although politics was not high on the agenda in the small villages the minutiae of parish level administration was important. The vestry minutes for Callington make mention of adjourning their meetings to one of the local inns, which would have been warmer and more comfortable than the unheated church. Our village inns would probably have been used for the same purpose especially as there were no competing meeting places until the latter half of the Victorian era, when schoolrooms at the National School or the Methodist Sunday School became an option.

The innkeeper, whose custom was limited in small parishes, would take every opportunity to encourage groups and societies to meet at his inn. Although the *Butcher's Arms* at St. Ive was on a turnpike road and perhaps had more custom than other small parishes, the St. Ive Friendly Society frequently met there. More important meetings would be publicised in the local newspaper and when the valuer acting in the matter of the "Inclosure of Saint Ive Down formerly called Silva Down or Penhergate Down" called a meeting at the *Butcher's Arms* in January 1850[WB], one can imagine that it would have been well attended and provided a welcome boost to trade for the landlord.

Auctions and Sales
The local inn was frequently used by auctioneers for sales of property, timber and even livestock. From the earliest newspapers in the eighteenth century, right though into the twentieth century, the village inn is advertised as the location of the survey and auction. There are mentions of auctions in Pillaton from 1762 and in St. Ive and St. Mellion from 1766[SM] and Stoke Climsland from 1722. It would appear that the innkeeper often acted in an additional capacity as adverts for properties in St. Ive mention that the landlord would show the property. In March 1863[CT] when some woodland at Trebeigh was for sale interested parties could "for viewing, apply to Mr. Olver at the *Butcher's Arms Inn*". Later that same year, in June, William Olver could be approached for viewing the 280 acre estate of Trebeigh when it came up for rent. Farms and estates regularly came up for rent on seven to fourteen year leases, so auction day would be of great interest to many in the parish, who would come to see who was going to be their new neighbour.

Fairs and markets

Although fairs and markets are associated with market towns such as Callington, some fortunate villages were privileged to have a charter for their own fair. Such fairs meant abnormal business for the only inn, as well as the crowds of people attending there would also be traders needing accommodation.

Pillaton was one such village which had a royal charter, an advertisement in the 'Sherborne Mercury' of April 1797 provides the details; "Pillaton Fairs will be held, according to the charter of King Charles the Second, on the 1st. and 2nd days of June, and on the 21St. and 22nd days of November yearly; which by being so near to Plymouth, the Dock, and other towns, will be worthy the attention of farmers, graziers, and others". Although the cattle market was the prime business of the day, other pleasures were long anticipated and most workers were given a day off. A 'West Briton' article of 1846 described the Truro Whitsun fair "Every body appeared to be on the tiptoe to see all that was to be seen, and a great deal there certainly was of the usual things exhibited at fairs, such as dancing shows, wild beasts, dwarfs, wax work, Punch and Judy, and all those other odd and comical things which people who go to fairs expect to see. Then there was also "Cheap John" duly in his place at the corner of a street, vociferating with the whole strength of his lungs concerning the cheapness of his wares, and the sacrifices he was making for other people's benefit". The article continues describing the noise from all the music and variety of stalls with "gingerbreads, comfits, nuts, sugar-sticks". Whilst Pillaton would not draw the same numbers, the attractions would be similar with traders and entertainers also coming from Plymouth.

St. Ive also had its own fair which was held in the field behind the *Butcher's Arms*. It is said that the charter was actually awarded to the inn and that it was displayed on the wall, until a recent landlord removed it when he left, taking with him the details of the original charter. The 1856 Post Office directory states that "A cattle fair is held on Thursday following the 8th of April" and Lakes Parochial History of Cornwall [1868] refers to "A fair is held at the Churchtown in April". The fair, or market, as it was then called, survived into the 1950s.

Games and Sport

According to H L Douch in his 'Old Cornish Inns', "The inn, and more particularly the brandy-shop were the homes of "card-playing, dicing and gambling which flourished to excess in the eighteenth century". When the justices finally clamped down on the worst excesses of carding and dicing there was still an occasional shuffle-board chamber for amusement and billiards became a new vehicle for gambling". We have no evidence of billiards in local inns but there are recollections of shuffle board being played.

One game we do know was played in the area is skittles. In Cornwall this was often called keels or kayles, In 1602 Richard Carew when writing about tinners noted that when they were not working hard "they weare out at Coytes, Kayles, or like idle exercises".[4] In 1762 at the Liskeard law-court the jury presented "the landlords in this borough that keep publick keeling alleys that are a great nuisance to the inhabitants, keeping servants and apprentices from their master's service and desire that they may be forthwith suppressed".[5] Skittles continued to be considered a nuisance to some of the population into the nineteenth century, but innkeepers promoted the game and instigated challenge matches between inns. In April 1859 a 'Cornish Times' correspondent when complaining about the state of Gunnislake referred to "skittle alleys are left open till 12 or 1 o'clock, to the annoyance of the whole neighbourhood". In 1841, on the tithe map, a small field behind the *Butcher's Arms* at St. Ive is clearly marked as 'skittle ground'. Stokeclimsland had a covered skittle alley at the *Half Moon Inn* in 1853 and the refurbishment of the *Cornish Arms* in St. Dominic in 1860 mentions a 'Kayle Ally'.

Being a country area the village inns benefitted from the country pursuits of foxhunting, coursing and horse racing. In the nineteenth century fox hounds belonging to the gentry frequently met in the area, with Viverdon Down, lying between Callington and St. Mellion being a favourite location. In the 1830s Mr. Phillips' hounds met at Viverdon, in the 1840s it was Mr. Archer's hounds, in the 1840s and 1850s it was Mr. Horndon's hounds who also met in St. Ive village and in the 1860s Mr. Raby's hounds worked the area. We do not know whether the meet for Viverdon was at the *Butcher's Arms* in St. Dominic, the *Sun Inn* at St. Mellion or at Pentillie Castle. Whichever inn had the privilege of hosting the hunt would have made the most of the extra custom. The hunt continued to meet at local inns into the twentieth century as a 1930s photo inside the *Butcher's Arms* indicates. Hare coursing was also a popular sport with Lady Edgcumbe mentioning it her journal in 1872[6] and Joe Snell still regularly coursing on the downs in the 1920s.[7] Whilst fox hunters imbibed at the start of the hunt, the followers or harriers, being on foot, would definitely have required liquid refreshment after a day coursing.

Another activity that would obviously have been well-supported was horse racing. Viverdon Downs was a popular location. Our clue to what had been happening was given in the 'West Briton' of September 1856 which refers to "leave had again been given by Col. Coryton of Pentillie Castle for races ... A Committee was appointed, the bill of racing printed, and circulars issued to different gentlemen". But Coryton, writing to Mr. Spry of Callington, one of the promoters, rescinded his permission after pressure from "the clergy of the neighbourhood" because "on former occasions it has led to drunkenness and every other immorality". This indicates that licensed premises in the neighbourhood had taken every opportunity to sell their wares at such functions.

The Pillaton Inn

Of the three old inns in this chapter, the *Weary Friar* at Pillaton appears to be the most likely candidate for having been a mediaeval church house because of its close proximity to the parish church of St. Odulphus. However no documentary or archaeological evidence of this has so far been found. Local lore is that it was originally built as accommodation for the masons working on the church, the oldest existing fabric of which dates from 1259. Henderson[8] suggests that there had been an earlier church on the site which would have been "a manorial church established after the conquest for the Domesday manor of Pilatona". Whatever the date, Pillaton has certainly had a church of some sort since the early mediaeval period, and it is therefore quite possible that a church house would also have existed.

For most of its existence the inn at Pillaton was known as the *Royal Oak*. It was not until 1963 that the then landlord, Geoffrey Cawthorne, changed its name to the *Weary Friar*. It has never been a tied inn, but remained in the ownership of the local lords of the manor, the Coryton family, and was part of the Newton Ferrers estate, until the estate was sold off in 1924. The name *Royal Oak,* is most likely to have been used for the first time in the second half of the seventeenth century following the restoration of the monarchy in 1660, the name being a reference to the Oak tree in which Charles the second is reputed to have sheltered from the Roundheads during the Civil War. Sir William Coryton, [1579-1651] of West Newton Ferrers, the local landowner during and after the Civil War was a prominent supporter of the royalist cause, despite his own personal puritan sympathies,[9] and his local tenants would no doubt have followed his example. It was certainly known as the *Royal Oak* by the middle of the following century when a land survey took place there in July 1762[SM]. By March 1842[WB], the landlord was Benjamin Sambel, who combined running the pub with trading as a butcher. Perhaps his was one of those common partnerships where the husband carried on a trade and the wife, in this case his wife Elizabeth, ran the pub, perhaps with the assistance of their young female servant Mary Wolkey. They would have had their hands full as the family also had three children under ten.[CS] It looks as if fortune did not favour the Sambel family. In March 1842 a thief stole "a box containing five pounds and upwards of money [comparable to £385 in 2010], sundry papers and other articles"[WB] from his home at the *Royal Oak* and Sambel was no longer at the pub by the time of the next census when John Smale appears as the innkeeper. By that time Mrs. Sambel was dead and Benjamin Sambel was merely an agricultural labourer living with his youngest daughter aged nine and a son of four. Life seems to have improved for him in the end, because in 1854 he married again and the marriage registers list him as having returned to his former trade of butcher.

John Smale seems to have had more success as an innkeeper, running the *Royal Oak* for over twenty years with his wife Susanna. He continued to combine innkeeping with another trade, this time he was the local grocer as well as the village innkeeper. The grocery business seems to have been run jointly with the pub for the next forty years, first by the Smales, then for a few years by Joseph Betty and

The Royal Oak in the shadow of the parish church, circa 1940-1950. The 'Central Stores, Pillaton' is in the foreground, with signs promoting Lyons Tea. CHC Ref: 2009.614.001

finally by Samuel Veale and his wife Thomasine until 1890.[CS] When Betty took over in 1872 the licence transfer records that the ratable value of the *Royal Oak* at the time was £13.

James Tucker was Innkeeper for a few months in 1890 but was soon superseded by William Pearce, a local man who combined his innkeeping with farming for almost thirty years until his death. Pearce and his wife Grace would have been another very busy innkeeping couple as they had six children living with them at the time of the census in 1891, including their adult daughter Caroline who no doubt helped in the pub. In Pearce's entry in the 1891 census the words 'licensed victualler' appear underneath his entry after his original description as publican and farmer. It is impossible to know who made this addition but we can speculate that he wished to make himself appear more respectable or more important than the term publican might suggest. It also suggests, as one would expect given its age and history, that the *Royal Oak* at that time served food as well as drink. Apart from this hint there is nothing to tell us what sort of establishment the *Royal Oak* was over its long history until its description in a sale catalogue of 1924 when the *Royal Oak* was sold as part of the sale and dispersal of the Newton Ferrers estate. At that date it comprised a "bar, bar parlour, two good sitting rooms, kitchen, dairy, and six bedrooms above together with garden and yard". Outside there was an "open Linney, Coal house, Cider Store, Stabling of Three Stalls, and One Loose Box". It was clearly a reasonably substantial property by that date, offering food and accommodation including stabling for guests' horses. If it had indeed been established since the mid-seventeenth century or before, it is most likely that it had always been a respectable establishment, serving food as well as drink and it probably provided accommodation for much of its history. It is unlikely to have been a common alehouse, serving only beer. On the other hand, the customers of the *Royal Oak* were not always sober – in May 1885 several of them were fined for drunkenness[WB]

Pearce himself seems to have been a relatively wealthy small farmer as well as running the *Royal Oak*. According to the sale catalogue of 1924 he was tenant of a number of "valuable enclosures" of land in and around Pillaton. William Pearce appears in the records for the last time in Kelly's directory of 1914. After that F.B.Pearce is listed as the publican in the 1923 directory. The sale catalogue of 1924, however, still refers to the tenant as being William Pearse who held the property on the yearly tenancy "at a low rent of £14 per annum". Pearce would have been over seventy by then so it may be that F.B. Pearce was William's son, Francis, who appears in the 1891 census as a scholar aged twelve. He may have taken over the running of the pub although his father remained the landlord.

The freehold of the *Royal Oak* was bought by the Balsdon family in 1924. Initially the landlord was Walter Balsdon but from 1930 until 1939 his wife Alice is listed as landlord as well as freehold owner. The pub changed hands ten times in the next forty years until Geoffrey Cawthorne took over as freehold owner and landlord in 1963 when he changed the name of the pub to its current name of the *Weary Friar*.

Today the *Weary Friar* remains as it has always been, the only pub in the parish of Pillaton. There is no longer a school or a village shop and the pub is the centre of village life for many residents. It still offers food for locals and visitors and accommodation for travellers. Both internally and externally its appearance is that of the traditional village pub and its current landlords, the Bakers, advertise on their website that you should "come to this famous old 12th century inn ... if you want solid comfort and a feeling of things as they used to be. ... here you will find real atmosphere and the unselfconscious dignity of great age".

LOT 33.

(Coloured GREEN on Plan No. 2.)

The "Royal Oak" Inn

(Free House),

Being Stone built, Detached and situate in the Village of Pillaton

Area 28 Perches

or thereabouts.

Part No. 178 on Plan.

Accommodation: Bar, Bar Parlour, Two good Sitting Rooms, Kitchen, Dairy, and Six Bed Rooms above, together with Garden and Yard.

Outside: Open Linney, Coal House, Cider Store, Stabling of Three Stalls, and One Loose Box.

Let to Mr. Wm. Pearce on a yearly Michaelmas Tenancy at the low rent of £14 per annum.

Tenant paying Rates and Land Tax.

Description of the Royal Oak from the 1924 Sale Catalogue for the Newton Ferrers Estate, CHC Ref: 1995.013.007

The St. Mellion Inn

St. Mellion is like Pillaton in that its pub, The *Coryton Arms,* is the only inn in the parish, and as far as we can discover this has always been the case. As with Pillaton, the records suggest that the inn was owned from its earliest days by the Coryton family and again like Pillaton its ancient name only changed in the late twentieth century. The *Coryton Arms* was originally the *Sun Inn,* a popular name throughout Cornwall and probably dating from the eighteenth century when inn names first appeared in any significant number. The inn existed before then but, like many similar village inns, probably had no name or sign and would usually have been known merely by the name of the landlord.

The *Coryton Arms* is less likely than the *Weary Friar* to have been a Church House. It is not immediately adjacent to the church, although it is still close enough being just across the road from the church and its immediately surrounding land. The road through St. Mellion would have been no more than a cart track in the middle ages and would not have been the obstacle to villagers which the current A388 is today. The existing building is not old enough to have been the church house as it dates from the early seventeenth century. Originally it had three rooms downstairs with a through passage and stairs to the first floor.[10] We do not know whether it was a purpose built inn [perhaps built to take advantage of the increasing traffic coming through the village on the road between Plymouth/Saltash and Callington/ Launceston] or whether it was originally built as a house, perhaps with one room for the inn which gradually took over more of the building.

The earliest evidence we have discovered for the existence of an inn in St. Mellion is a lease dated 23rd May 1674 under which a John Treneer junior of St. Mellion, 'victualler' rented some land from Sir John Coryton of West Newton. Where there was a victualler there must have been an inn, so we can assume that John Treneer was one of the first, if not the first, landlords of the building we know today. After that the records are silent for over a hundred years apart from an advertisement of January 1766 in the 'Sherborne Mercury' for a survey which was to take place at 'the house of John Kennar, Churchtown, St. Mellion'. As we have seen such surveys were an early form of auction and often took place at the local inn. The Kennar family were certainly connected with the inn by the early 1800s. In September 1804 the "public house called the *Sun*" in St. Mellion was leased by a Matthew Kenner of St. Mellion from John Tillie Coryton of Crocadon, for fifty years at a rent of £15 per annum. However Matthew Kenner is described in the lease as a yeoman, [and in an endorsement on the lease as "Mr. Kenner - Yeoman"]. 'Mr' was a term which at that date still indicated a farming status above that which one would expect of an innkeeper, so it is unlikely that Matthew Kenner ran the inn himself. He probably sublet to his own tenants, as did William Horndon of Callington, for example, who leased the *Three Cranes* and the *Wellington* in Callington from Lord Baring but sublet to the actual innkeepers. Intriguingly, however, Matthew Kennar is described as 'husband-man' in other documents – a tenant farmer below the rank of yeoman, and a more likely description of the type who would become a village innkeeper or indeed run an inn alongside his work as a husbandman. The first is a lease of 1780 of a "house in St. Mellion" which was 'formerly' held first by John Kennar and then by John and Matthew Kennar. John Kennar was Matthew's father[11] and almost certainly the house owner of 1766. John Kennar himself was described in a lease of 1756 as a 'husbandman' and both John and Matthew are described as 'husbandman' in the 1780 lease. However Matthew appears in the St. Mellion marriage registers as just a 'labourer' in 1781 when he married his wife Elizabeth at St. Mellion on 22nd February. As we have seen in an earlier chapter, not only were occupations described in a fairly loose way, but often an innkeeper would

The Sun Inn, St. Mellion from a postcard of circa 1900

have a dual occupation and his description in documents might not mention that he was also an innkeeper. The most likely solution is that Matthew's father John was the head lessee of the inn and originally the innkeeper as well, but probably combining his innkeeping with small time farming. The family then seem to have prospered, perhaps because of the increase in travellers on the road to and from Callington, so that by 1804 when Matthew renewed his late father's lease of the inn from John Tillie Coryton he was able to describe himself as a Yeoman and by that time he almost certainly sublet the *Sun Inn*. We do know from an endorsement on the lease that 'Mr. [Matthew] Kenner' did not die until 2nd August 1831. There were several named 'victuallers' at the inn in the intervening years, details which seem to confirm that Kenner sublet the inn to tenant 'victuallers' who ran it for him.

The first of these was William Herring, mentioned in two surveys which took place in May 1796 and March 1797 "at the house of William Herring, victualler, St. Mellion".[12] It looks as if William Herring was dead by the turn of the century because two surveys were held in 1803 and 1804 "at the house of Mary Herring, victualler". She was almost certainly his widow,[13] running the pub on her own account after his death.

James Rickard is then named as victualler in surveys held at the *Sun Inn* between 1809 and 1812 and in 1813 he is described as 'innkeeper' in the baptism record of his son Stephen and again in 1821 when he took on an eleven year old apprentice. John Smale was apprenticed to help Rickard with 'husbandry'[14] showing that Rickard was also a dual occupation innkeeper/farmer. Perhaps the inn was run by his wife Susanna and their daughter, also called Susanna, until her marriage in 1822 to Thomas Nanscawen a husbandman. The *Sun Inn* certainly seems to have been very much a family affair. After James Rickard died, in 1830, Susanna's husband Thomas Nanscawen took over the running of the inn. He appears in the 1841 census as a 'publican' living in St. Mellion with Susanna and their seven children plus his mother in law Susanna Rickard then aged sixty five and his brother in law William Rickard aged thirty. Nanscawen also appears to have kept up the farming activities of his predecessor landlords – he appears in all his children's baptism and marriage records as 'labourer'.

Nanscawen was still at the inn at the time of the 1851 census, this time described as a 'victualler' aged fifty two, living with his wife Susannah and four daughters aged between seven and seventeen. Nanscawen's mother in law, Susanna Rickard,was still alive but living next-door and described as a pauper. The Rickard/Nanscawen families do not seem to have done as well out of the Sun Inn as their predecessors the Kenners. Nanscawen probably

died in 1857 by which time his wife Susannah was already dead and the inn was briefly run first by an R. Bate whose only reference is in Harrods directory of 1856 and then by George Harris who appears briefly as innkeeper in the 1861 census when he is recorded as being a farmer and innkeeper aged sixty-three living with his wife Mary aged sixty-four.

Thomas Davey was the next innkeeper and although his initial lease from Augustus Coryton in March 1867 was for only one year [at a rent of £23 to include the inn and five acres of fields],[15] with the advent of Davey, The *Sun Inn* once again became a family affair. In the 1871 census Davey is recorded as being a "licensed victualler and farmer of six acres" aged forty-six, living at the *Sun Inn* with his wife Mary and three children aged under seven together with a female 'general domestic servant' aged thirteen. Davey is so far the only St. Mellion innkeeper to whom we have found reference in the newspaper reports of licensing sessions. In September 1869[CT], Captain Horndon reprimanded Davey for his conduct at the inn and warned him that if the case had been left to him he would have refused to renew the licence. Reading between the lines it seems that Davey only escaped because of the presence on the same licensing bench of his landlord, Colonel Coryton. The licence was however transferred to Thomas's wife Mary in 1875, so Horndon may eventually have had his way, but it is more likely that it was because Davey had died. He was certainly dead by March 1878 when Mary Davey married George Solomon and both parties were described as widowed. George Solomon had previously been the village policeman but he took over the licence of the *Sun Inn* from Mary Davey in 1878 and by 1881 the census records him as living there as licensed victualler aged thirty-eight, with his wife Mary [Thomas Davey's widow] two of Mary's children aged seventeen and eleven, and George's four children aged between four and thirteen. Mary died in 1895, aged sixty-four, but George Solomon remained the innkeeper of the *Sun Inn* for over forty five years and after him Mary's son, Anthony Davey took over until about 1930. *The Sun Inn* was thus in the hands of one family for over sixty years.

Records of the rent over those years suggest, however, that the inn was not prospering. In 1882 a note written on the original lease to George Davey records that the rent was being reduced. From 1882 Solomon was paying £12 per annum for the inn and £10 per annum for the attached fields. In 1907 a further note records a reduction in rent to 30d, which seems to suggest that times had become very hard indeed.

By 1930 the long tenure of the Davey/Solomon family had come to an end and Kelly's directory records that William H. Bond was the innkeeper at the *Sun Inn*. From then on, the story is similar to that of the *Royal Oak* at Pillaton and the inn changed hands many times during the rest of the twentieth century. It was sold off from the Coryton estate and the name was eventually changed to the *Coryton Arms*. It is still the only pub in the parish and *'The Corrie'* remains a popular local pub under the current landlord, Trevor Hewson.

The St. Ive Inn

The inn at St. Ive village, currently known as the *Butcher's Arms*, claims to be a sixteenth century inn. Of the village inns featured here, this inn is the least. likely to be a church house, as it has never been on glebe land. A short distance to the west of the inn and the church is Trebeigh, an estate that has had a considerable influence

The Butcher's Arms, St. Ive, 2010. The old mounting block can be seen near the left corner of the building, providing a platform for some plant pots The single storey extension that was the butchery can just be seen on the right

on the parish since the time of the 'Domesday Book' [1086]. It was given to the Knights Templar in about 1150 and then in the fourteenth century to the rival order of St. John of Jerusalem or Knights Hospitallers. The first Rector under the Knights Hospitallers was Bartholemeo, and he was the one who had much to do with the construction of the church as we know it today. It was rededicated by the Bishop of Waterford in 1338. In 1350 the Bishop refused to allow the parish church of St. Ive to be appropriated to the Hospitallers, though they continued to have the tithes. Henry VIII in 1536 ordered the dissolution of the Monasteries, and transferred all Hospitaller properties to the Crown. In 1587 the estate passed into the Wrey family who retained it for nearly 400 years.[16]

Both orders of Knights had a reputation for hospitality and would have provided refreshments and accommodation for the infrequent travellers along the Callington to Liskeard road. What ale-houses may have existed in the village prior to the dissolution is unknown. If the current inn is sixteenth century as claimed, it may have been built after the dissolution, when a private family took over Trebeigh and no longer provided hospitality to travellers. The inn stood on land owned by the estate until it was sold to a brewery in 1898. Sadly the bulk of the records of the Wrey family were destroyed in a house fire in the nineteenth century, so the only possibility of proving the age of the current inn may be the charter for the fair mentioned above.

The public house is Grade II listed, and according to English Heritage it is considered to be circa seventeenth century. Local residents state that the single storey building on the east side of the inn used to be the butchery/slaughter house. On the west end of the front elevation there is a mounting block as a reminder of when many clients would arrive on horseback and may have needed a little extra help to get back into the saddle when they left!.

In the latter half of the eighteenth century there are newspaper references to auctions and surveys. In 1766 and in 1783 the 'Sherborne Mercury' refers to surveys at the "house of Charles Blake, Churchtown, St. Ive". No name is given for the inn until 1796 when there is a survey "at the sign of the *Cornish Volunteer*, St. Ive Churchtown". In the last decade of the eighteenth century, with the threat of a French invasion and an expansion in the local voluntary militia, the *'Volunteer'* was a popular and patriotic name. It is possible that, prior to this period, the inn at St. Ive may have had another name or just have been referred to by the innkeeper's name. Charles Blake died in 1812 and is buried in St. Ivo's churchyard having passed away at the age of eighty-seven. He may well have retired before his death, but it is not until 1819 that we know the name of another landlord. John Chapman was landlord from at least 1819 until 1841. In October 1840 the lease of the inn was advertised for auction. It was called *'The Butcher's Arms'* and John Chapman was the occupier. It comprised; gardens, stables, brew-house, slaughter-house and courtlage. This indicates that John Chapman was a butcher and he may have been the first butcher at the property and responsible for the change of name.

By the time of the 1841 census in April of that year, William Olver was in occupation. William originally came from St. Germans and his wife Jane from Menheniot. By the 1851 census they had six children and one servant. It is only in an 1856 directory that William describes himself as an innkeeper and a butcher. He later describes himself as an innkeeper and farmer of sixty acres. By the 1871 census his son, also called William, is shown as a butcher and has a separate entry in an 1878 directory. William senior, retired in 1888 and died in 1891 at the age of seventy-five years. The next publican was Harry Bolitho who took over the licence on the 5th July 1888[17] he was also a butcher. Harry stayed at the inn until 1898 when it passed from the ownership of the Rev. Bourchier Wrey to the Plymouth Brewery. William Alford took over as licensee and was followed by George Oliver and then John Emmerson who stayed until nearly 1950. Bill Batten took over from John and stayed for nearly forty years. After he left there has been a regularly changing list of landlords. Some recent landlords have been 'characters' with one going bankrupt and boarding himself into the inn for about six months. His successors also went bankrupt, but business has improved with the present licensees, Angie and Gordon Clark who have been at the inn since 2006.

Bodminland/Pensilva

St. Ive is not such a small parish as St. Mellion and Pillaton. For centuries it was clustered around churchtown and the road to Callington, an agricultural village in the middle of a large agricultural parish. In the nineteenth century a completely new village sprung up, on the most unlikely ground on the edge of the parish. This was Bodmonland or Bodminland, built on the edge of the moors mainly to accommodate miners, from the 1840s onwards. As can be imagined inns and beer shops arose to meet the needs of the miners. At one time there was a *Commercial Inn,* a *Miner's Arms* and the *Victoria Inn,* and probably a good handful of illegal beer shops! John Scoble was at one time the licensee for the *Miner's Arms* which eventually lost its licence in 1860 due to "irregularities". In the 1861 census John Scoble was at Victoria Farm, and in September 1862 a "new licence was granted, viz., to the "*Victoria Inn*, Bodmon Land, kept by Mr. Scoble".[CT] The *Victoria Inn* is the only inn to survive in Pensilva from the mining era.

The Village Inn Today

For centuries the village innkeeper had to survive serving the local, and often small population. They often did this by having two occupations, one for the day and one for the evening. The boom time for the village inn was when ownership of the motor car expanded and excursions out into the country were a popular activity, thus considerably increasing the client base of village inns. This continued into the latter twentieth century and innkeepers responded by beginning to provide food as well as liquid refreshment. Today there is hardly a public house that does not provide food, but in the twenty first century everyone is well aware of the danger of drinking alcohol and driving and this has now reduced the custom to village inns. Once again publicans in small villages have to diversify to survive.

In 2001 HRH the Prince of Wales launched "The Pub is the Hub" initiative. As he said "The country pub, which has been at the heart of village life for centuries, is disappearing in many areas. Providing services from the pub, such as a post office or a shop, keeps an essential service in the village". In Stratton the *Tree Inn* absorbed the local post office when this was closed. At a time when local post offices and shops are closing at an alarming rate it is unfortunate that this initiative has not had a better uptake. Whilst the catering at the *Weary Friar*, Pillaton and the Who'd *Have Thought It*, St. Dominick manages to attract additional custom from groups, what will the *Butcher's Arms* and the *Coryton Arms* have to do to ensure their survival in this century?

Superscript abbreviations
CT   Cornish Times
SM   Sherborne and Yeovil Mercury
GAZ   Royal Cornwall Gazette
WB   West Briton
DR   Street or Postal Directory
CS   Census information

1. Eamonn Duffy, *The Voices of Morebath*, Yale University Press, London, 2003
2. Duffy, p.109
3. David Hey, ed. *The Oxford Companion to Local and Family History*, Oxford University Press, 2002, p.236
4. Richard Carew, *The Survey of Cornwall,* 1555-1620, 1st edition, London 1602
5. H L Douch, *Old Cornish Inns*, Bradford Barton, Truro 1966. P.59
6. Journal of Lady Ernestine Edgcumbe, 19th Jan. 1872 RIC, DJE/1/1
7. Natalie Allen, *Full Circle*, Saltash, 2000, p.39
8. Charles Henderson, *Cornish Church Guide and Parochial History of Cornwall*, D. Bradford Barton Ltd., Truro, 1964, pp.165-6
9. See for example, Anne Duffin, *Faction and Faith: Politics and Religion of the Cornish Gentry before the Civil War*, Exeter University Press, 1996; Mark Stoyle, *West. Britons: Cornish Identities and the Early Modern British State*, Exeter University Press, 2002
10. English Heritage listing description, 1985
11. Lease, 1780, Cornwall Record Office [CRO] CY/2399
12. CRO CY/5719 and CY/5837
13. St. Mellion parish registers record the marriage of William Herring and Mary Sweet in November 1787
14. CRO P188/14/20
15. CRO CY/2602
16. Ann Eade, *Spotlight on St. Ive* October 2008 newsletter of the Callington Heritage Centre
17. Register of Licences CRO/JC/EMMID/26

Index

Act, Alehouse 1552   53
Act, Beer, 1830   8, 13, 21, 29, 40, 48
Act, Commutation 1784   25
Act, Defense of the Realm 1914   28
Act, Food and Drug 1875   26
Act, Licensing 1552   7
Act, Licensing 1872   11, 29, 40
Act, Licensing 1904   10
Act, Licensing 1921   13
Act, Licensing 2003   12
Act, Sale of Beer 1854   29
Act, Wine & Beerhouse 1869   9
Acts 1604-1627   7
Adam, James   18, 53
Adamson, George   59
Adit The, Calstock   58
Albaston   17, 34, 54, 56, 61-62
Albion Arms, Drakewalls   61
alehouse   5-8, 27, 55
aletaster   53
Alford, William   36, 80
Allen, Natalie   69, 70, 71, 72
Alman [Almond], William   54, 57, 59
Ancient Order of Buffaloes   56
Annie's Cafe, Callington   42
Archbishop Aelfric   6
Archbishop Manning   27
Archer, Mr.   74
Ash, John R   57
Ashburton Hotel, Danescombe   52, 57, 59, 62
Ashburton, Lord estate   41, 42, 48
Ashton, St. Dominick   65, 67
Assembly Rooms, Callington   22, 27, 37
Aubyn, Sir John St.   13
auctions - see also surveys   10, 37, 41, 48
    56, 65, 71, 73, 77, 79
Aunger, Henry   18
Babb, James   36, 42
    Les   28, 69
Baber, St. Dominick   15, 68
Back Lane, Callington   33, 39
Ball, John   49
Balsdon, Walter & Alice   76
bands , [musical]   22, 28, 48, 51, 56, 63
Bands of Hope   23, 27, 28, 52, 55
Baptist Street, Calstock   58
Barbican, Plymouth   9, 70
Baring estate   36, 38, 77
barley   15, 16, 53
Barnes, Superintendent   11, 52
Bassett, Harry   47
Bate, R   78
Batten, Bill   80
Batten, Misses Caroline, Florence   27
Battle of Hastings   5
Battle of Waterloo   38

Bazeley, Rev. F L   22, 24
Bealswood [Bellswood] Inn, Netstakes   60
beer   8, 10, 12, 14, 15-17, 19, 21, 22, 26, 27
    28, 48, 53, 69, 71, 75
beer shops   8-13, 21, 24, 40-43, 45-48, 50, 52
    55, 60-62, 67, 70, 80
beer, ginger   25
Bennett, Edmund   71
Bennett, James G   71
    John   67
    William   51
Bennetts, Mr.   47, 51
Bethel Methodist Chapel, Golberdon   47
Betty, Joseph   75, 76
Bible Christians   23, 30
Bickle, John   16, 41, 61
    William   61, 62
Binley, Andrew   52
Bishop Brewer of Exeter   6
Bishop of Waterford   79
Blake, Charles   79
Bligh, Richard   18
Blue Cap Hotel, Callington   36, 38, 44
Bluc Ribbon Movement   28
Blundell, C W & Co.   36
Boatman's Arms, Calstock   54, 57
Bodiner, John   51
Bodmin   6, 21, 22, 23, 24, 32, 59
Bodminland [Bodmonland] *now Pensilva*   80
Body, Joseph   38, 39
    Stephen   62
    Susan   39, 43
    William   41
Bohetheric[k], St. Dominic   15, 16, 71, 72
Bolitho, Harry   80
Bolt, James   52, 59, 79
Bond, Abraham   59
    Benjamin   68
    William H   78
Bond's Commercial Hotel, Callington   33, 35, 36
Bond's Hotel, Gunnislake   59
Bonman, H   46, 50
Boot Inn, Calstock   59
Booth, Charles   27
Borlase [Burlace], William   54, 57
Boundy, Luke   47
Bowden, Jimmy   19
    Robert & Caroline   36, 58
    William G   42
Bowhay brewery/family   17, 47, 48, 58, 59, 61, 62
Bowhay, Edward   34
    Nick   34
    Thomas T   17, 34
Box, Ellis   16
Bray Shop   45, 46, 50
Bray, Peter   8

Brent, William 16
Brevan, Robert 58
Brewery, Bedford 59
Brewery, Blundell C W & Co. 36
brewery, breweries 8, 10, 11, 16, 17, 24, 29
36, 38, 42, 43, 47, 48, 49, 53, 58, 59, 61, 71, 79
80
Brewery, Courage 10, 36
Plymouth 10, 11, 38, 42, 49, 80
St. Austell 71
Tamar 10, 17, 36, 61
Tavistock 47
brewing 6, 10, 12, 16, 17, 36. 41, 53, 57, 69
brewster sessions 52, 59, 60, 63, 69
Bridge Inn, Gunnislake 61
Bridgman, Mr. 60
Broad, William 59
Brooklands Farm, Metherell 16
Brown, John & Jane 35, 42
Buccaneer Inn, Gunnislake 60
Buckingham, Mrs. 42
Budge, James 39
Bullen, Henry 9, 34, 35, 40
Buller's Arms, Liskeard 21
Bull's Head, Callington 13, 17, 31-35, 37, 40
42, 44
Burlace [Borlase], William 54, 57
Burley, Robert 51
Burnham, Francis 36
Burnham, Henry 63
John 63
Butcher's Arms, Albaston 62
Butcher's Arms, St. Dominick 67, 69-71, 74
Butcher's Arms, St. Ive 73, 74, 79-80
Callington 4, 7, 8, 9, 10, 11, 12, 13, 16, 17
21-30, 31-44, 51, 52, 54, 59, 61, 62, 68, 71, 73
74, 77, 78, 79, 80
Callington Church of England Temperance Society
28
Callington Cricket Club 34
Callington Ringers 42
Callington Temperance Society 28
Callington Total Abstinence Society 28
Callington United Temperance Society 28
Calstock 4, 16, 17, 18, 19, 22, 25, 27, 28
33, 43, 51-64, 69
Calstock Inn, St. Ann's Chapel 54, 62
Camelford 31, 35
Camp, George H 62
Caradon 21, 22, 23, 31
Carew, Richard 6, 7, 14, 66, 72, 74. 80
Carpenter, Thomas 34
Carpenter's Arms, Metherell 53, 54, 57, 62
Cassell, John 26, 27
Catherine of Braganza 25
Cawthorne, Geoffrey 75, 76
Central Control Board [Liquor Traffic] 1915 12
Chamberlain, George & Jane 49
Chapman, John 79, 80
Cheesewring 24
Chilcott, Mr. 72

children 6, 12, 13, 14, 19, 23, 28, 33, 46
47, 48, 50, 60, 65, 66, 69, 75, 76, 78, 80
Chilsworthy 18, 28, 55, 56, 62, 63
Chilsworthy Brass Band 64
church ales 6, 7, 34, 73
church house 6, 34, 45, 47, 73, 75, 77, 79
Church Street, Callington - *see also Lower Street*
30, 33, 39
Chynoweth, William 16
cider 15-19, 21, 22, 24, 46, 53, 56, 76
Cider House, Stoke Climsland 46
Clark, Angie & Gordon 80
family 45, 46, 50
Rev. Ed. 13, 37
John 16, 62
Clenic, S 46
Coachmaker's Arms/Inn, Callington 17, 30, 35
41-42, 44
Coad, Mr. 49
Coath, Robert 62
W 62
Coath's Hotel, Albaston 62
Cock, David 35
John 58
cockfighting 7, 73
Cocking, Cattern 67
Joseph 63, 64
Thomas 52, 63, 64
coffee 5, 8, 10, 26, 27
Cole, Police Constable 51
Collin, Fred 19
Colling, Mr. 61
Colling, Thomas 54
Commercial Hotel, Bond's, Callington 33, 35, 36
Commercial Hotel, Calstock - see *Naval &*
Commercial Hotel
Commercial Hotel, Gunnislake 59
Commercial Inn, Bodminland 80
Commercial Road, Calstock 57
Commercial Street, Gunnislake 55, 60
Congdon Margaret 39
Griffin 65
Mary 15
Samuel 65, 66
Congland, Margaret 39
Constabulary, policing, parish constables 10, 11
Coode, Mr. 41
Copeland, Reuben 63
Cornish Arms, St.Dominick 17, 54, 65-69
Cornish Arms/Inn, Gunnislake 54, 57, 59, 61, 74
Cornish Volunteer, St.Ive 79
Cory, John 57
Coryton Arms 13, 77, 78, 79, 80
Coryton family 74, 75, 77, 78
Cotehele House/Quay, Calstock 16, 17, 19, 41
53, 61, 62, 69
Cotehele Mill, St. Dominick 66
Country House Inn, Harrowbarrow 62
Cousens, John & Mary Ann 70
Cox Park 56

Crabb, James 34
    Richard 15
    William 39
Cradick, George 69
    Richard 70
Crober, Mary 66, 67
Crocadon, St.Mellion 77
Croker, Richard 27
Crook, John 62
Cross, [Monk's Cross] Stoke climsland 28
Cross, St. Dominick 67, 70, 71
Crosskey, Callington 43
Crown Inn, Callington 39, 40
Crow's Nest, St.Cleer 21
Danescombe, Calstock 52, 59
Davey, Anthony 78
    George 78
Davey, Mr. 49
    Thomas & Mary 78
David, John 39
Davies, Dr. D S 25
Davis, Philip 34
Davy, Miss 34
Daw[s], Peter 60
Dawe, John 26
    Susan 62
Delbridge, George & Mrs. 30, 42
Devonport 23, 38, 58, 67, 70, 71
Devonport Inn, Calstock 58
Diamond, John 67
Dimond, Thomas 67, 70
Dingle family 39
    Edward 16
    Jeffery 34, 39
    John 43
    Sarah 39
    William 30
Dodd, George 52
    Maggie 56
Doidge, Albert 63
    John 46, 47
    Richard 15, 61
Downing, Police Constable 68
Drakewalls 61
drunkenness 6-14, 15, 21-24, 36, 51, 52
    58-60, 62, 68, 69, 75, 76
Duke of Cornwall's Arms, Calstock 54, 56, 57
Duke of Wellington 8, 38
Durber, Edwin & Mary Ann 57, 59
Dustan, William 35
Dymond, Police Constable 42
Edgcomb, John 15
Edgcumbe Ams, Cotehele 16
Edgcumbe, Earl of Mount 66, 69, 70, 71
Edgcumbe, Lady 74
Eggsford, John 46
Elliot, Andrew 16
Elliott, Police Constable 56
Emmerson, John 80
Exeter 6, 32
Eyre, T S 25
fairs 31, 39, 41, 68, 69, 71, 74, 79

Fairweather, Robert 38, 42
Falmouth 32
farmers 12, 13, 15, 16, 17, 19, 22, 24
    31, 36, 39, 46, 48, 50, 51, 53, 59, 61
    62, 63, 65, 67, 70, 74, 76, 77, 78. 80
Farmer's Arms/Inn, Golberdon 13, 48-50
Farnham, Surrey 11, 49
Fletcher, Michael 18
Floyd, Samuel & Thomasin 46, 47
Foot, Isaac 49
Fore Street, Callington 32, 33, 35, 36, 38, 42, 43
Fore Street, Calstock 58
Forester's [Forrester's] Arms, Callington 30, 31
    39, 41, 42, 43, 44
Forester's Arms, Gunnislake 61
Fountain Inn, Callington 38, 42, 44
Francis, William 46
Fraser, Robert 19
Free Hotel, Albaston 62
Friendship, John 65, 66, 69
    William 70
Gadgecombe, James 18
Geach, Jacob 16, 37
    William 15
George, Temperance 52
Gerrans, John 39
Ghey, Sidney & Vera 35
gin 8, 9, 13, 14, 15, 21, 69
ginger beer 25
Golberdon 13, 28, 47-50
Golden Lion, Devonport 38
Golding family 12, 13, 33, 36, 37, 38, 42, 47
Golding Hotel 22, 27, 33, 36-38, 42, 47
Gooseford, St. Dominick 68
Great Exhibition 25
Gregory, George 43
    William 63
Grigg family 45, 46
Grubb, Johane 15
Guildhall, Callington 36
Gumb, John 46, 47
Gunnislake 17, 22, 23, 27, 28, 52, 53
    54, 57, 59-61, 62, 69, 74
Half Moon Inn 45-47, 50, 74
Halfway House, Polbathic 71
Halton Barton, St. Dominick 16, 71
Halton Manor, St. Dominick 15, 16,17, 65
Halton Quay, St. Dominick 17, 19, 67, 71
Hambley, Joseph 66
Hambly, John 67
    Richard 32
Hampt, Stoke Climsland 18
Hare and Hounds, Callington 43
Harris, Arnold 62
    George 16, 78
    Jacob 61
    Samuel 62
    Thomas 15
Harrison, Brian 29, 30, 40
Harrowbarrow 27, 28, 53, 55, 62, 67
Harrowbarrow Working Men's Club 62
harvest 15, 18, 19, 21, 24, 55, 56,59

Harvey, John		60
Harvey, Robert		45
Harvey's Hotel, Gunnislake		60
Hatt		71
Hawkey, John		36
Hawkins, John & Mary		67
William		67
Hawton, Thomas		71, 72
William		45
Hayes, James		36
Hearder, G P		71
Heathfield, St. Dominick		18
Hender, John		15, 65
William & Phebe		65
Henwood, Linkinhorne		10, 23
Henwood, John		62
William		36
Herring, John		56, 57
Mary Ann		70
William & Mary		78
Hewson, Trevor		78
Hicks, Sarah		10
Higher Metherell Inn, Metherell		62
Hill, Thomas		58
Hingston Down		31, 63
Hockaday, Mr. & Mrs.		72
Hodge, Joseph		60
William		38
Hodge's Hotel, Gunnislake		60
Holmbush Mines		31
Honeycombe, Richard		53
Hornabrook, Mr.		34
Horndon, Cptn.		78
David		36, 43, 74
William		77
Horrill, Prudence		18
Horsebridge		47
Horswell, Mr.		23
Hughes, Leonard		70, 71
Hullah, Thomas		51
Humphrey, George		42
Hunn, Clarence		53
Samuel		53, 62
hunting		38, 70, 74
Hutchings, John		17, 57, 58
Hutchins, Henry		43
Jackman, William & Elizabeth		58
Jaggard, Edwin		16
Jago, John		40
Jagoe, Thomas		18
James, Edwin		58
Elizabeth		34
Joseph		62
Silas		43
Jane, Alberta Maude		59
James H & Alberta		59
Joan		15
Richard		16
William		15
Jasper, Sampson		36, 41
William		42, 60
Jenkin and Co.		25
Jennings, Albion		83
Jewell, John		52, 63
Thomas		52
Johnson, William		60
Johnson's Hotel, Gunnislake		60
Joll, John		17
Jope, James		34
kayles, keels		68, 74
Keast, Edward		34, 40
Robert		43
Kelly Bray		31, 43, 47
Kelwa, Alice		15
Kenner, John		77
Matthew & Elizabeth		77, 78
kidleywinks		9, 40
King Charles II		8, 25
Edgar		5
Ethelbert of Kent		5
George V		12
Henry VII		7
James I		7
King, Police Constable		72
King's Arms, Bray Shop		46, 47, 50
King's Arms, Callington		39, 40
Kirk, David		26
Kit Hill		27, 31, 33
Kneebone, Edward		18
Knight, Elizabeth		66
Knights Hospitaller		79
Knights of St. John		79
Knights Templar		79
Knill, George		16
Knoydart House, Church Street		39
Lake, Thomas		36
Lakeman, George		35
Landulph		19, 41
Lane, Coffin		19
Lang, Samuel		69
Langman, John		57, 58
Joseph		54, 57
Thomas		57
Langsford, Peter		19
Latchley	18, 19, 23, 26, 51, 52, 55, 59, 63	
Latchley Hotel/Inn Latchley		63
Launceston	6, 22, 25, 31, 32, 43, 77	
Lawrence, John		62
Lawrey, James C		58
Lawry, James		19
Laws, John		35
Lea, William		51
lemonade		25
licensing sessions	8, 9, 10, 41, 42, 52, 78	
Linkinhorne	17, 46, 50	
Liskeard	8, 21, 22, 24, 28, 31, 32, 33, 62, 74, 79	
Little Dale Farm, Latchley		63
Livesey, Joseph		22
Lobb, Nathaniel		43
London	9, 13, 25, 26, 27, 71	
Looe		22, 31
Lord, William		46
Lower Metherell Inn, Metherell		62

Lower Street [Church St.], Callington 30, 31
33, 39, 40, 42, 43
Lucas, Alice 65, 69
Mary 66, 68, 69
Richard 67
Robert 66, 67, 68, 69
William N 17, 67, 68, 69
Luckett 17, 18, 28, 45-47
Maddeford, Richard 45
Maders 17, 48, 49
mail coach - *see also post coach* 32, 33
Maker, Arscott 36
Malachi, Joseph 58
maltster 15, 16, 17, 39, 46, 59, 61
Maltster's Arms, Luckett 17, 46, 47, 50,
Maltster's Arms, Halton Quay 67, 71
Market Hotel, Gunnislake 60
Market House Inn, Callington 17, 30, 36, 42, 44
Market Inn, Gunnislake 17
Market, Pannier, Callington 36
markets 22, 31, 33, 39, 41, 74,
Marshall, Police Inspector 43, 68
Martin, Benjamin 39
Bob 17
Marion 17
Richard 71
Stephen 17, 67, 71
Thomas 17, 36, 42, 69
Walter 47
Martyn, Alfred 55
Marke 18
N 34
Mason, Sarah 71
masons 61, 67, 75
Mason's Arms, Gunnislake 60
Matthew, John 39
Matthews, Richard 62
May, Richard & Mary Ann 42, 43
W J 71
McGuffin, William 26
measures [of drink] 46, 53
Menheniot 69, 80
Merrel, Charles 64
Metherell, [Metherhill] Calstock 16, 17, 52, 53
54, 57, 62
Methodists 24, 26, 29, 30, 39, 42
44, 47, 49, 50, 52, 73
Methodists, Bibile Christian 23, 30
Methodists, Plymouth Brethren 60
Methodists, Primitive 23, 24
Methodists, Wesleyan 24, 27, 28, 30, 42, 63
Millet, John 52
Milroy, John 26
miner 21, 22, 31, 36, 40, 44, 47, 48, 50
51, 52, 55, 61, 62, 63, 68, 71, 80
mineral water - *see water*
Miner's Arms, Bodminland [Pensilva] 80
Miner's Arms, Latchley 63, 64
mining 21, 22, 23, 31, 33, 43, 48
50, 51, 55, 71, 72, 80
Minions 21

Mitchell, David 58
Hannah 58
William 58
Moon, Theophilus 40
William 34
Morden Mill, St. Dominick 67
Morebath, Devon 73
Mortimore, Mr. R 36
Morwellham 17, 23
Mudge, Dr. Henry 22
James 55, 62
Mutton, Ann 15
Nanscawen, Thomas 78
William 17
Nattle, William 70
Naval and Commercial Hotel, Calstock 17, 25
57, 58
Neblett, William 61
Netstakes, Calstock 52, 60
New Inn, Callington 32, 33, 34, 36-37, 40
New Inn, Calstock 17, 52, 58
New Inn, Golberdon 47-50
New Inn, Stoke Climsland 45
New Road, Callington 32, 37, 38
Newbridge Inn, Callington 43
Newbridge, Callington 43
Newbridge, Gunnislake 32, 62, 62
Newport Inn 16, 41
Newton Ferrers, Pillaton 75, 76, 77
Newton, Calstock 16
Nichols, Richard 60
Nicolls, Mr. E 52
Norden, John 7
Normans 5, 7
Normington, Catherine 61
John 71
Northey, Henry 62
Northey's Hotel, Albaston 62
Okehampton 26, 31, 32
Old Clink, Callington 35, 36
Oliver, George 80
Olver, William 73, 80
Orford, Earl of 37
Lady 35-37
Oxford Inn, Harrowbarrow 62
Padstow 23
Parkin [Perkin], William 16, 46
Pasteur, Louis 27
Paul, John & Elizabeth 39, 62
Peake, William 47
Pearce, F B 76
Grace 76
Mr. 49
Samuel 72
William & Grace 72, 76
Pearse, Mary 18
Samuel 57
William 76
Pencrebar, Callington 43
Pengelly, Jane 60
Penharget Down, St. Ive 73

Pensilva - *see also Bodminland* 23, 27, 28, 48, 80
pensioners 13, 48, 49
Pentillie Castle 74
Pepper's Hill, St. Dominick 66
Perkin [or Parkin], William 16, 17, 46
Peter, Mr. 52, 63
Peters, James 43
    Ann 41, 42
    William 43
Pethick, Richard 13, 48, 49
Phillips, Mr. 74
Philp, E 26
    Simon 16, 45, 46, 50
Phoenix The, Callington 35, 36, 44
Pidgeon, Rev. A 52
Pillaton 73, 74, 75-76, 77, 78, 80
Pine, James 67
Piper, Richard 51
Pitt, William the Younger 25
Playing Place, St. Dominick 66
Pledge, The 22, 23, 28, 52, 56
Plymouth - *see also Brewery, Plymouth* 8, 9, 19
    25, 31, 35, 36, 42, 54, 55, 69, 70, 71, 74, 77
Plympton 58
Plymstock 17
Poad, John 67
Policing, parish constables 10, 11
Pomeroy, Stephen 41
Pomery, Walter 12
Pomroy's shop 36
porter 22, 27, 36
Porter, William & Ann 12, 32-37
post coach 32
postal service 31
post-chaise 32, 33, 34, 37
Potter, Drew & L 70, 71
    Eddie & Lily 71
pottle 5
Potts, John & Elizabeth 65
    Thomas 65, 66
Poundstock 6
Preston, Lancashire 22, 24
Pridham, Gerald 20
    Mac 56
    Roger 19
priests 5
Primitive Methodist 23, 24
Prince of Wales 80
Procter, Nicholas 16, 41
    Thomas 57, 58
prohibition 27, 29
Prospect Farm, Latchley 19
Prout, Joseph & Susan 57, 62
Quakers 23, 57
Queen, Elizabeth I 19
Queen's Head, Albaston 17, 56, 61, 62
Quethiock 28
Rabbage, James 70
Raby, Mr. 74
racing 24, 71, 74
Radland Mill, St. Dominick 66
railway 25, 31, 33, 43, 55, 60

Railway Inn ,Kelly Bray 31, 43
Rapson, Mary Ann 34
Read, Thomas 17
Rechabites 23, 55
Red Lion, Callington 31, 32, 34, 35, 39, 41
Redmoor Mines 31
Register of Licenses 42, 43
Rendell, Robert 42
Rich, John 47, 48, 65
Richards, Harriet 55
Rickard family 78
    Hannah 62
    Henry 71
    John 57
Rifle Corps Inn, St.Ann's Chapel 62
Rifle Volunteer, St.Ann's Chapel 54, 56, 62, 63
Rilla Mill 23, 28
Rilla Mill Teetotal and Band of Hope Society 28
Ring O Bells, Callington 16, 30, 38, 39, 44
Ring O Bells, Stokeclimsland 16, 46, 47, 50
Rising Inn, Latchley 51, 63, 64
Rising Sun, Gunnislake 60
Rising Sun, Maders 48-50
Roberts, Inspector 52
    John & Betsy 58
Rogers, Jack 71
    John 62
    Joseph 47
    Mr. 49
    Thomas 57
Roseveare, Sergeant 68
Roughtor 24
Rowe, James 16, 46, 58
    John 16
Rowell, Thomas 48, 49
Rowse, William 46, 47, 50
Royal Oak, Callington 30, 36, 41, 42, 44, 47
Royal Oak, Gunnislake 32, 61
Royal Oak, Pillaton 75, 76, 78
Rundle [Rundell], William 35
    Henry 34
    Richard 51
St. Agnes 24
St. Ann's Chapel 17, 32, 54, 56, 62-63
St. Austell 23, 24, 32
St. Columb 32
St. Dominick 13, 15, 16, 17, 18, 19, 22, 23
    24, 36, 37, 42, 65-72, 73, 74, 70
St. Dominick Fair 71
St. Dominick Reading Rooms 28
St. Germans 80
St. Ive 27, 27, 28, 43, 67, 71, 73, 74, 77-80
St. Ive Friendly Society 73
St. Mellion 13, 73, 74, 76-78, 80
Saltash 31, 33, 35, 49, 58, 77
Saltash Road, Callington 27, 37, 42
Sambel, Benjamin & Elizabeth 75
Sanders, John 61
    Robert 36
Sargeant, Robert 38
Sargent, George & Emma 17, 36
    J 39
    Nicholas 37

Satchell, John 58
Saxons 5
Scawen, Thomas 65
Schweppe, J J 25
Scoble, John 80
Searle, James & Amelia 59
Sheffield Cottages, St. Dominick 70, 71
Sheffield The, St. Dominick 70, 71
Silva Down, St. Ive 73
Sims, George 21
Skinner, Ezekiel 15
 James 46, 50
 John 25, 58
Skinnerd, Richard 15
skittles 45, 56, 63, 74
Slade, John 16
 Richard 16
Sleep, Simon 47
Smale, Henry 58
 John & Susanna 75, 78
 Shirley 57
 William 58
Smeaton, St. Dominick 71
Smith, Charles 67, 69
 John 65
 William & Elizabeth 65
smuggling 8, 25
Snell, Joe 74
 William 42
Solomon, George 13, 78
 William 39
South Hill 33, 45, 47-50
South Hill Band 48
South Hill Friendly Society 48
South Ward Lead Mine 57
Southey, Alexander 39
Sowden, R 46, 50
Spark, Frances 71
Spear, John 42, 67, 68
Spettigue, Stephen 52, 58
Spry, Mr. 74
stables, stabling 16, 31, 32, 35, 36, 37, 39
 41, 42, 43, 45, 57, 63, 66, 69, 76, 79
Steam Packet Hotel, Calstock 58
Steed, William 62
Stephens, Agnes 18
 Bill 28
 Mr. 55
 William 51, 59
Stockwell, St. Dominick 15
Stoke Climsland [Stokeclimsland] 16, 19, 27, 28
 33, 41, 43, 45-50, 62, 73, 74
Stoke Damerel, Plymouth 42
Stratton, Bude 19, 59, 80
Strick, Joseph 61
Stroud, Sir George 33
Sun Inn, Callington 17, 39, 44
Sun Inn, St. Ann's Chapel 63
Sun Inn, St. Mellion 74, 77, 78
Sunday Opening/Closing 8, 13, 29
Sunday Schools 23, 27, 73

surveys 7, 15, 19, 37, 40, 42, 45, 54, 59
 61, 62, 63, 65, 68, 73, 75, 77, 78, 79
Symonds, Henry T 58
Symons, Capt. 41
 John H 59
 Nicholas 18
Tamar Inn, Calstock 17, 54-58, 62
Tamar Inn, St. Dominick 23, 71, 72
Tamar River/Valley 15, 17, 18, 19, 21, 31
 32, 59, 61, 71
taverns 5, 7, 8, 27, 55, 64
Tavistock 17, 31, 32, 59, 60, 61
Tavistock Arms/Hotel/Inn, Gunnislake 17, 52, 54
 55, 56, 59, 62
Taylor, Robert 49
Teare, James 23, 24
Temperance Hotels 27, 55
Temperance Society, Callington 9, 22, 28
 Calstock 27
 Devonport & Stonehouse 23
 Gunnislake 27
 Harrowbarrow 55
 Liskeard 22
 Pensilva 27
 St. Ive 23
 Truro 9, 22, 24
Thorne, John & Co. 32
Thornton, Rev. F V 38
Three Cranes, Callington 32, 34, 36, 39, 77
Tibb, Elizabeth 18
Tibbs, Tristram 15
tipling houses 6, 7
tipplers 16
Tipwell, St. Dominick 67
Toll, John 16
Toms, John 42
Towell, St. Dominick 17, 69
Town Arms, Callington 39, 42
travellers 5, 7, 8, 31, 32, 36, 37
 60, 73, 76, 78, 79
Trebeigh, St. Ive 73, 79
Tree Inn, Stratton 80
Tregoning, Mr. 51
Treise, R & Charles 35
Trelawney, John 15
Treloar, Robert 63
Trematon Castle 18
Trenavin, Golberdon 49
Treneer, John 77
Trevarton, George 52
Trewin, George 67
Trotter, Thomas 8
Truro 9, 22, 25, 32, 33, 46, 74
Tucker, James 76
Tucker, John 47
turnpikes 32, 35, 37, 54, 56, 59, 61, 62, 73
Tywardreath 72
Uglow, W 25
Under Lane, St. Dominick 70
Under Road, Gunnislake 60
Under Road, Gunnislake 60
Veale, Samuel & Thomasine 76

Venning, James	25-28, 38, 59	Wesley, John	26
Vernigo, St.Dominick	66	Wesleyan Methodists	24, 27, 28, 30, 42, 63
vestry meetings	23, 24, 33, 34, 41	Westcott, St. Dominick	15
	65, 67, 68, 69, 73	Westlake, Ben	38
Victoria Inn, Bodminland	80	William	71
Victoria Inn, Calstock	58	White Hart, Callington	34, 39, 40
Viverdon Down	74	White Hart, Chilsworthy	62, 63
Vivian, Henry	35	White Horse, Callington	39, 40
Vosper, George	62	White, Mrs.	54, 62
John	26	White's Temperance Hotel, Gunnislake	54
Vyvyan, Elizabeth	35	Whitley, Joseph	33, 37, 40
Wadebridge	31	Who'd Have Thought It, St. Dominick	67, 70, 71, 80
Wadge, Agrippa	34	Whyta, Radulf	53
Wakem, Henry	62, 63	widows	12, 18, 21, 32, 34, 35, 36
James	63		37, 39, 41, 42, 43, 45, 46, 47
Thomas	62		48, 57, 58, 60, 65, 66, 69, 78
wakes	5	Willcocks, George	60
Wall, John	70	Williams Town - see also Gunnislake	59
Ward, Joseph	58	Williams, Charles	35
Warrick, John	51	Cptn.	64
water	6, 14, 15, 17, 21, 25, 38, 51, 53	Frederick	55
water, carbonate	25	Joseph	57, 58
water, mineral	25, 42, 58	wine	5, 9, 15, 22, 24, 37, 40, 42
Waterman's Arms, Calstock	54, 57	Winsor Arms, Kelly Bray	43, 46, 47, 50
Wearing, William	36	Winter, Samuel	33, 34
Weary Friar, Pillaton	75-77, 80	Wolkey, Mary	75
Webber, Doris	17, 71	Woolridge, Henry	47
Webster, David P	55	Worgan, G B	18
Well Lane [Street], Callington	27, 39, 42	World War, First	12-14, 28, 35, 55, 58, 62, 69
Wellington Inn, Callington	30, 32, 38, 39	World War, Second	17, 35, 47, 60, 62, 63
	42, 44, 77	Worth, John	48, 49
Wellington, Duke of	8, 38	Worth, Samuel	55, 62, 68
Wenmouth, John	31, 41	Wrey family	79, 80
Werring, Mr.	34	Wright's Hotel, Callington	43

This book has been published by the Callington Heritage Centre. All profits from sales go towards the continuing maintenance of the artefacts and archive of the Centre. The Centre was established in 1984 by the people of the town for the preservation of the heritage of the town and the surrounding area. Since that date it has been entirely managed by volunteers for the benefit of the community and visitors from further afield.

The Heritage Centre is in Liskeard Road, Callington and is open from Easter until the end of October, on Fridays, Saturdays and Sundays between the 1000hrs and 1600hrs, subject to their being sufficient volunteers stewards. The Centre welcomes visitors to our annual exhibitions and for research purposes, entry and use of all facilities is free to everyone. Local residents wishing to be involved in research projects or willing to assist with stewarding are always welcome. Please contact the Centre by email on enquiry@callingtonheritage.org.uk or telephone 01579 389506 and leave a message.

OTHER RECENT PUBLICATIONS

Edwardian Callington. A snapshot of what life was like in Callington and the surrounding area during the Edwardian era [1901-1910]. Lavishly illustrated with photos and advertisements from the period.

Callington Doctors, The Medical History of a Cornish Town. Through tracing the development of the medical profession in Callington and the surroundings areas from 1675 to the present day, it is possible to understand what facilities were available to the ordinary family, in health and in sickness.

Both available from Callington Heritage Centre